THE INVISIBLE HOMELESS

THE INVISIBLE HOMELESS
A New Urban Ecology

Richard H. Ropers, Ph.D.

Southern Utah State College
Cedar City, Utah

 **INSIGHT BOOKS**
Human Sciences Press, Inc.

Library of Congress Cataloging in Publication Data

Ropers, Richard H.
   The invisible homeless: a new urban ecology.
      p.   cm.
   Bibliography: p.
   Includes index.
   ISBN 0-89885-406-7
   1. Homelessness—United States.   2. Homelessness—California—Los
Angeles County.   I.   Title.
HV4505.R66 1988
362.5′0973—dc19   87-23286
                                                                    CIP

For my children, Libby and Ryan.
May they never have to lose their dreams.

CONTENTS

ACKNOWLEDGMENTS

The research on the homeless population of Los Angeles was conducted by the author as a National Institute of Mental Health post-doctoral scholar, (NIMH Grant No. T32MH14-664), in the Psychiatric Epidemiology Program at the School of Public Health, University of California, Los Angeles (UCLA), and as founder and co-director of the Basic Shelter Research Project, UCLA. Dr. Michael Goldstein, Dr. E. Richard Brown, Dr. Emil Berkanovic, Dr. Michael Vojtecky, and Richard Boyer, M.A., all of the Division of Behavioral Sciences and Health Education, School of Public Health, UCLA, played a role in advising the research and/or writing parts of this book. Richard Boyer assisted in the writing of Chapter 1 and in the computer analysis.

I wish to acknowledge the permission of the executive director of the Single Room Occupancy Corporation to analyze and use the corporation's data on the Los Angeles SRO residents.

The numerous volunteers who worked as interviewers and coordinators in the various data collection stages have made this book a truly communal product.

Mary Ann Dolcemascolo provided invaluable assistance in making this work come alive through her photography and her dedicated research.

Mona Lee Harris deserves great credit for putting up with me while she assisted in interviewing homeless organizer Ted Hayes and touring the Los Angeles skid row. Her photographs are also gratefully appreciated.

I also gratefully acknowledge the input to various chapters of the book by attorney Gary Blasi, chair of the homeless litigation team, Legal Aid Foundation of Los Angeles, who is also a member of the executive committee of the National Coalition for the Homeless, and by Theresa Rubin, a licensed clinical social worker, who is project director of Transitional Living and Community Support, Sacramento. Dr. Robert Slayton of the Chicago Urban League suggested thoughtful changes to Chapter 2.

I am honored that my former professor and my friend, Dr. Larry T. Reynolds, wrote a foreword and reviewed the entire manuscript. To have my work enhanced by the preface by Dr. Richard Appelbaum is also a privilege. His detailed criticisms and reviews have been instructive to me.

The experience I have had as the live-in manager of the Care and Share Shelter, Cedar City, Utah, has provided me with a deep sensitivity to the plight of my fellow Americans who are homeless.

Ted Hayes, an organizer of the homeless, deeply moved me with his vision and devotion. Ted gave up time to personally give me a tour of Los Angeles' skid row and spent generously many hours with me so that I could interview him.

A special thanks to Bonnie Mitchell, director of the Multicultural Center, Southern Utah State College, whose friendship helped me through some difficult personal times during the writing of this book.

Janet Seegmiller was much more than a word processor; she played a vital role in editing, and my many conversations with her helped sharpen my thoughts and their expression.

Norma Fox, editor-in-chief at Human Sciences Press, was very receptive to the possibility of this book, and I gratefully acknowledge her efforts and those of her staff in making it a reality.

Various aspects of this book have appeared as articles or research documents, and I would like to acknowledge those journals and institutes and their permission to use my previously published work: the Intergovernmental Relations and Human Resources Subcommittee of the Committee on Government Operations, U.S. House of Representatives; the University of California, Institute of Governmental Studies; the Urban League of Chicago; the U.S. Department of Health and Human Services; and the *International Journal of Social Science and Medicine*. Thanks also to the publishers for permission to quote from the following books: Riis, J. (1890). *How the other half lives* (pp. 86–87). New York: Charles Scribner & Sons.
Lamb, H. R. (Ed.). (1984). *The homeless mentally ill: A task force report of the American Psychiatric Association* (pp. 182–184, 213–214). Washington, DC: American Psychiatric Association.

Finally, I am moved by the dignity of the many homeless persons who shared their stories with me. This is truly their book.

FOREWORD

The Tragedy of Homelessness

Homelessness is nothing new, but it is also nothing less than a major tragedy—and it is a tragedy that looms large in our times. There are more homeless in the United States today than at any time since the Great Depression. Homelessness affects millions, and the problem increases dramatically, week by week, month by month, and year by year. Before the decade of the 1980s draws to a close, homelessness will envelope still more of the millions of our fellow citizens who are currently unemployed; millions more, whether they realize it or not, stand but a paycheck or two away from the same fate.

Many of the homeless do, however draw paychecks, though the paychecks are inadequate to pay for a room, to say nothing of an apartment or a house. In fact, of those 33.7 million Americans who lived in poverty in 1984, fully 40 percent were gainfully employed. By that year the gap between the poor and the rich in this country had become wider than at any time since 1947, the year that data on income distribution first began to be collected by the U.S. Bureau of the Census. Since 1984 the gap has not lessened; rather, it has increased, and homelessness is a direct consequence of this growing social inequality; a formidable array of evidence attests to the fact that homelessness is not a product of individual failure. Nevertheless, in spite of the evidence, "victim blaming" explanations of homelessness dominate both the popular and the social science literature on the topic. To realize how grossly inadequate are all such victim-blaming explanatory frameworks, one need only examine just who they are who make up the ranks of today's homeless.

The widely held and seriously mistaken view is that the homeless are mainly derelicts, alcoholics, bag ladies, the physically disabled, and the mentally ill. "Bums," "winos," and "crazies" are out there all right, but they hardly constitute the majority of those with no place to hang their hats. They have been joined by single men, young women, children, and whole families. They have also been joined by the unemployed, the underemployed, the seasonally employed, and in some cases the fully employed. Unlike previous generations of the homeless, today's, especially in urban areas, are younger, better educated, and have more stable employment histories. A higher percentage are females, veterans, and/or minority group members, and they have been homeless for shorter periods than their counterparts in previous generations.

The composition of the homeless population of the United States in the 1980s indicates that homelessness is not a private problem but rather what C. Wright Mills termed a public issue. And that is precisely how Richard H. Ropers deals with it. He refuses to adopt the conventional victim-blaming perspective; from his thoroughly sociological vantage point, homelessness is not the result of individuals' shortcomings but the expected by-product of the structure of present-day society. Ropers does not focus on the personal characteristics of the homeless when he seeks an explanation of the changing composition of their ranks or the dramatic increases in their numbers. Instead, he examines sociological variables such as deindustrialization, slashed welfare programs, shortages in low-income housing, increased poverty rates, economic recessions, and the economic policies of the Reagan administration.

Among the many advantages enjoyed by his approach when compared to that of the "victim blamers," not the least is that Ropers can point the way to a real solution. In the long run we do not need more shelters for the homeless, nor do we need more soup kitchens—what we do need is a major shift in the balance of political power in this country, leading to a radical restructuring of our economy. Victim-blaming analyses of the homeless will do nothing to solve the problem; what will help us solve it are more well-done works like *The Invisible Homeless*.

Larry T. Reynolds, Ph.D.
Vice-President
North Central Sociological Association

PREFACE

This volume offers significant insights into the origins and nature of homelessness in America. Combining extensive personal experience with tough-minded analysis of survey research data, Richard H. Ropers debunks one of the prevalent myths concerning homelessness—that people are homeless primarily because of some form of personal disability. Through interviews with homeless people in shelters, soup kitchens and single room occupancy hotels, Ropers determines that today's homeless differ significantly from those of the recent past. Contrary to the 1950s image of the homeless as elderly, white, male, skid row alcoholics, the homeless of the 1980s tend to be younger and disproportionately minority in origin. More are female, and entire families are included. Alcoholism, substance abuse, and psychological disabilities are far less common among the homeless than one might expect, especially given their adverse living circumstances. As Ropers demonstrates, homelessness today results in large part from economic adversity. One would have to go back to the Depression and Dustbowl of the 1930s to find a parallel.

In a society that emphasizes achievement through individual initiative, lack of success is commonly attributed to personal failing. This "blame the victim" attitude is found in popular culture and is frequently legitimated by what passes for scientific knowledge, as the most common explanations for homelessness tragically illustrate. It is widely believed, for example, that people are homeless by choice, because of laziness, or because they are unwilling to control their intake of drugs and alcohol. A slightly more sophisticated analysis, advanced by many in the mental health profession, treats homelessness as the result of a complex interrelationship between substance abuse and psychological malfunction. Insofar as the latter interpretation views the underlying causes as beyond the immediate control of the individual, it is presumably the more sympathetic of the two. But both versions have this in common: they look to the causes of homelessness in the individual rather than in society itself.

If homeless people are indeed responsible for their plight, how does one explain the rapid increase in homelessness, particularly among women with dependent children? Has the number of irresponsible or psychologically disturbed people really increased in recent years—especially among female-headed families? Clearly not. There must be another explanation for the growing incidence of homelessness in the United States. Ropers convincingly demonstrates that today's homelessness results primarily from economic and political, rather than personal, factors.

The restructuring of the U.S. economy has resulted in rising unemployment and declining wages, as formerly high-paying industrial jobs have fled to cheap foreign labor markets, replaced by lower-paying service sector employment at home. As the economy has deteriorated, the Reagan administration has responded by cutting back on virtually all social programs that serve the poor, from food stamps and welfare to housing. The combined effect of these cutbacks has been to shred the social safety net at the very time when growing numbers are badly in need of help. To make matters worse, the demand for rental housing has risen sharply over the past decade, as rising homeownership costs have pushed an ever-increasing number of persons into the rental housing market. At the same time, high interest rates and economic stagnation have contributed to a slump in rental housing construction. Rental housing scarcity, growing demand, and high interest rates have combined to make rental housing increasingly unaffordable. The gutting of housing allowances and public housing by the Reagan administration—and the administration's efforts to sell off much of the existing public housing stock—have exacerbated the problem.

Growing joblessness, falling wages, the reduction in government social programs, chronic low-income housing shortages, rising rents—these are the structural sources of homelessness. We should not be surprised to find a disproportionate number of substance abusers or mentally disturbed among the homeless; they are the least capable of dealing with adverse economic conditions and hence the first to succumb. And once they are on the streets, the experience of homelessness certainly contributes to their psychological and physical problems. But homelessness already extends far beyond this initial group, as it touches the working poor and occasionally even the middle class. Loss of a job or a spouse may result in failure to meet rent or mortgage payments. Suddenly the streets become an all-too-real possibility.

While the sources of homelessness may be numerous, ultimately it is society's unwillingness to guarantee adequate shelter that compels people to live in the streets. In the long run, the principle solutions to homelessness are to be sought in the larger economy, with adequate social programs for those who fail to benefit. But the simple truth is that if shelter were regarded as a right, there would be very few homeless in the United States.

How many homeless are there? Not surprisingly, there is little agreement on even this basic issue. In fact, few issues concerning the homeless have stirred up so much debate as this seemingly simple question. National estimates range from a low of 350,000, the official figure of the U.S. Department of Housing and Urban Development (HUD)[1], to a high of several

---

[1] US Department of Housing and Urban Development, *Report to the Secretary on the Homeless and Emergency Shelters* (Washington, DC: HUD Office of Policy Development and Research, 1984).

million, the figure preferred by advocates for the homeless and shelter providers. Numbers are extremely important, since they affect the willingness of government agencies to spend money on shelters, relief, and other programs. The major studies completed to date have been remarkably deficient in their estimation procedures—in the case of the HUD report, irresponsibly so. A brief examination of this latter estimate, which remains the Reagan administration's "official" homeless figure, provides insight into the political importance of numbers.

The HUD study is the first and, to my knowledge, the only study to date to attempt a truly systematic national survey of homelessness. Because of its official status and national scope, its low estimates have been particularly troubling to advocates for the homeless. A primary objective of the HUD study was to identify the special problems and characteristics of people in shelters and on the streets. Along the way, however, HUD decided that it first had to come up with a national estimate of the *extent* of homelessness, and that turns out to have been a bad decision. HUD used three methods to arrive at this figure, and the three methods suffered from similar problems. I will briefly present one of these approaches, to illustrate the chief error.[2]

HUD's research was based on interviews in 60 metropolitan areas, selected so as to constitute a national sample of three different size-strata of places (50,000–250,000; 250,000–1,000,000; and over 1,000,000). Shelter operators and other activists dealing with the homeless were interviewed using a "snowball" technique, whereby HUD hoped to identify all the experts in a given area and combine their various estimates in a sort of weighted average. The 60 metropolitan areas were in fact Ranally Metropolitan Areas, or RMAs—extremely large units developed by Rand McNally for use in its annual com-

---

[2] For a detailed analysis of the HUD report, see Richard P. Appelbaum, oral and written testimony before congressional hearings, House Banking Committee serial no. 98-91, May 24, 1984, and Banking Committee serial no. 99-56, December 4, 1985.

mercial marketing atlas.[3] Rand McNally defines RMAs as including:

> (1) a central city or cities; (2) any adjacent continuously built-up areas; and (3) other communities not connected to the city by a continuously built-up area if the bulk of their population [8 percent of the population or 20 percent of the labor force] is supported by commuters to the central city and its adjacent built-up areas. Rand McNally has identified 394 RMAs in the United States.

Since they include central cities and outlying suburbs, they cut across city, county, and in some cases even state boundaries.

This approach landed HUD in a methodological swamp, for it had apparently gathered estimates on homelessness for selected *cities*, and then proceeded as if those estimates applied to the much larger *RMAs.*—I say "apparently" because it was not immediately evident from the published report that HUD had in fact made this error; in fact, HUD did its best to obscure the origin and scope of its original estimates. On the surface, however, even HUD's published report provided ample grounds for skepticism, since a number of its RMAs were far too large to be surveyed by its handful of interviewers. For example:

> The New York City RMA includes some 74 cities in 24 counties across 3 states; it has a total 1980 population of 16.6 million people, of which New York City itself accounts for only 43 percent.
>
> Los Angeles, the second-largest RMA, is even more dispersed than New York, with 10.6 million people living in 88 cities in 5 counties; the Los Angeles City population is less than one-third of the total.
>
> The Chicago RMA has 7.8 million people in three states,

---

[3] *Commercial Atlas and Marketing Guide* (Chicago: Rand McNally, 1983), p. 87.

10 counties, and 46 cities, of which Chicago itself has only two fifths.

All told, HUD's 20 largest RMAs have a combined 1980 census population of 78.3 million, which amounts to one out of every three Americans. These RMAs are substantially larger than more conventional political units, such as counties and cities. For example, the combined population of the principal counties for each of the 20 largest RMAs is only half of HUD's combined RMA population, while HUD's combined central city population comprises only one-third. The 20 largest RMAs encompass 455 cities in 141 counties, across 32 states. This represents an average of approximately 7 counties and 23 cities per RMA. It is obviously of great importance to know whether the person interviewed believed himself or herself to be providing homelessness estimates for the entire RMA, the county, the city—or perhaps only the downtown "skid row" area.

Although HUD initially declined to reveal the detailed information on which its estimates were based, it was eventually possible to get access to the raw interview protocols for the 20 largest RMAs under the Freedom of Information Act. As revealed by this unpublished information, HUD arrived at its projections in the following way. The survey of "knowledgeable observers" began by asking, "How serious a problem is homelessness in your city?" No reference was made to RMA or even to metropolitan area; nor was any effort made to define "city." It is clear that the interviewee was not responding in terms of the RMA, a term that was never mentioned and in fact would not have been meaningful to interviewees, and so could be used. Therefore, the response necessarily refers to the much smaller city itself. For the 20 largest RMAs, only 205 completed questionnaires provided point-in-time estimates of homelessness, or about 10 per RMA. There is substantial variation in response rate, with Cleveland and Baltimore providing only 4 estimates each, at one extreme, and Los Angeles providing 35, at the other. Only 6 RMAs actually provided 10 or more estimates. How could HUD have covered one-third of the American population—living in 455 cities—with so few interviews?

Consider Boston by way of example. Reportedly, HUD derived its Boston RMA estimate from a half-dozen different sources—all of which, in turn, got *their* estimates from the same place, an Emergency Shelter Commission census that found 2,800 homeless person on the streets and in the shelters in October 1983. The study excluded abandoned buildings, dumpsters, parking garages, MBTA bus and train yards, most parked cars, and dead end alleys—as well as the Charlestown and West Roxbury areas. It should also be mentioned that the Commission told HUD interviewers that their own figure was a "gross underestimate,"[4] with 5,000–10,000 as a more accurate number. HUD chose to ignore this revised figure, and it used the 2,800 as if it applied to the greater metropolitan area, which includes virtually the entire urbanized New England seaboard—some 3.7 million people in 41 cities, 5 counties, and 2 states (Massachusetts and New Hampshire). The homeless outside of Boston were completely ignored, even though the city itself contains only 15 percent of the total RMA population. The same error was made in most of the cities HUD surveyed; HUD interviewed a handful of people in each city, who offered "guesstimates" of the number of homeless in the city itself; HUD then applied those figures to the surrounding RMA.

There is one major flaw in the HUD study that bears mention because it is endemic to all studies of homelessness: the difficulty, if not impossibility, of defining "homelessness" in a way that does not do a disservice to those who lack shelter. HUD limits its count to people sleeping on the streets or in emergency shelters. It explicitly excludes residents of halfway houses, congregate living facilities, long-term detoxification centers, and single room occupancy (SRO) hotels, and it also excludes people forced to sleep temporarily in someone else's residence because they have no alternative. Even within HUD's restricted definition, it is obviously difficult to locate people who avoid the authorities or who have lost their housing and wind up sleeping in cars, abandoned buildings, or on friends' sofas.

---

[4] City of Boston, Emergency Shelter Commission, *The October Project: Seeing the Obvious Problem* (Boston: the Commission, 1983) and *Census of the Homeless* (Boston: the Commission, 1986), p. 98.

I do not know whether HUD's undercount was an intentional effort to downplay the significance of the homeless problem, as some have asserted. However, it is clear that HUD's research was sloppy and poorly executed, producing hidden errors that HUD revealed only when forced to do so under the Freedom of Information Act, errors that HUD has subsequently never acknowledged.

Whatever the current number of homeless, there is no disagreement that the problem has worsened substantially in recent years. Nor does the near future seem especially hopeful. The economic conditions that have contributed to the problem are not expected to improve, at least in the near term. By now the structural problems of the American economy are well appreciated and much discussed by economists and policy makers. Nor does the enormous national debt portend well for a significant increase in social spending, particularly in the face of sluggish economic growth, declining tax revenues, enormous military expenditures, and the ever-present specter of recurring inflation. The 1986 Tax Reform Act removes much of the speculative value from rental housing, and this, at least in the short term, is expected to produce rent increases of as much as 25 percent. Nor is tax reform likely to encourage rental housing construction.[5]

Perhaps the best that can be hoped for at the present time is an enhanced understanding of the sources of homelessness and a willingness on the part of the government at all levels to provide for emergency relief. In the long run, however, the solution to homelessness necessarily lies in a major rethinking of national priorities concerning both housing and our treatment of the poor.

Richard P. Appelbaum, Ph.D.
Department of Sociology
University of California, Santa Barbara

---

[5] John I. Gilderbloom and Richard P. Appelbaum, *Rethinking Rental Housing* (Philadelphia: Temple University Press, 1987), Chapter 4.

INTRODUCTION

The homeless seem to be everywhere. Some are visibly homeless, like the bag ladies, the shopping-cart people, the disheveled who huddle in doorways, and others who seem to wander aimlessly in streets and alleys. And then there are the "invisible" ones, those who "pass." On the surface many of these are indistinguishable from the rest of us. Some roam shopping malls or the hallways of universities during the day. At night they try to rest in rat- and roach-infested all-night movie theaters, in lonely schoolyards, in their cars, on subways, or in the cold restrooms of public buildings.

The obviously homeless individuals, who seem to fit long-held stereotypes as bums, derelicts, winos, and the insane, are only the tip of the iceberg. Most of the contemporary homeless are difficult to detect because of their diversity and "invisibility." In public places many homeless persons attempt to keep up appearances as best they can in order to seek employment and gain access to public facilities like schools, libraries, shopping malls, and restrooms, where they rest and wash. Many others are borderline homeless, living temporarily with friends or relatives, in motels, or in single room occupancy hotels (SROs).

For example, a systematic survey commissioned by the *Los Angeles Times* concluded that there are 42,000 car garages sheltering about 200,000 individuals in Los Angeles County. The majority of these invisible "garage people" are immigrants from Central America and Mexico—it has been argued that they are mostly economic and war refugees of U.S. foreign policy. The report on the survey charged that many landlords profit from renting their garages, making as much as $450 a month from rent, and are often in violation of sanitation, safety, and zoning laws.

> One of these "garage people" described her situation: In Nicaragua we had a house, a TV. I had a bedroom. Now I cannot tell anyone where I live because I am ashamed. My father had to build a bathroom for us outside (Chavez and Quinn, 1987).

While many citizens are able to fulfill the American dream of material success and a meaningful life, others are living the American nightmare of homelessness. While the limited economic recovery has benefited those at the top of the stratification system, those at the bottom are still waiting for the benefits of the "trickle-down effect." In the meantime, our urban landscapes only show evidence of the trickle-down misery.

The new urban homeless of the 1980s constitute an underclass, literally out of sight. The problem isn't that we choose not to see them; we just see past them. Most of us try to avoid the homeless. If we encounter them on the street, we move away; we may even cross the street or change our direction. Psychologically, we try to put them out of our minds or rationalize away the causes of their condition. We are afraid to face them, because we may recognize our own vulnerability to economic and social insecurity. A mythology has emerged that would have us believe that the homeless are all "lazy, crazy, drunk, or doped." Some contend that the homeless freely choose their life styles and are simply modern-day gypsies.

To acknowledge who the homeless really are and where they came from raises questions about current economic and social policies; perhaps the mythology about the homeless is perpetuated to avoid this. We are not facing reality if we attribute personal failure to victims of decreases in available low-income housing, structural unemployment caused by the deindustrialization of basic industry, urban renewal, and cutbacks in social welfare. As long as "blaming-the-victim" explanations are given for homelessness in the United States, social policies based on such perspectives will fail to resolve the problem.

Not since the Great Depression of the 1930s have the soup kitchen lines been so long and the numbers of homeless Americans on the street so great. Research indicates that the new urban homeless of the 1980s are a diverse population that includes women, children, adolescents, single men, and families. A 1987 survey of 29 major cities found that the number of families requesting emergency shelter had increased by 31 percent in two years. This survey also concluded that one-third of the nation's homeless population consisted of families (United States Conference of Mayors, 1987, p. 1). The new urban homeless are younger, better educated, and disproportionately nonwhite compared with the homeless populations of the past. The majority have been homeless less than a year, and approximately half of the men in many cities are veterans of U.S. military service (Ropers & Robertson, 1984a; United Way, 1983; Ropers, 1985a). These new homeless have joined the ranks of the "skid row" denizens across the country, who are traditionally elderly, physically and mentally disabled, or alcohol or drug dependent.

The rise of a new homeless population is occurring in other Western industrial countries as well. Citing economic recession, high levels of unemployment, and insufficient public housing as causes of increased homelessness in Western Europe, a recent report indicates that there is no end in sight to Europe's growing homeless populations. England is estimated to have 100,000 homeless and France 600,000, while 400,000 homeless are reported in West Germany. The vast majority, 93 percent of the homeless in Western Europe are described as the "new poor." The "classic vagrants" of Europe are being dramatically replaced by homeless families with children and young unemployed men (Tuohy, 1985).

In the early 1970s, social scientists wrote about the disappearance of skid rows and skid row populations; today, however, skid rows are not only re-emerging but overflowing. The skid row way of life is no longer confined to a particular geographical location, but has become a condition that permeates our cities. This modern syndrome, of skid row as a condition and not a place, is symptomatic of what may be a deep structural urban crisis confronting our cities.

Social services for the homeless are completely inadequate. Neither the private nor the public sector meets the shelter, medical, food, and employment needs of the homeless. The federal government estimates that on any given night emergency shelters across the nation can provide only 111,000 beds; 12,000 of these beds are for runaway youth and another 8,000 for battered women (HUD, 1984). In Los Angeles County, which has been designated by the U.S. Department of Housing and Urban Development (HUD) as having one of the largest homeless populations (33,800) in the nation, there are only about 3,500 private-sector emergency shelter beds (Blasi, 1987). More homeless persons die of hypothermia (exposure to the elements) in "warm and sunny" Los Angeles than in New York City (Clem, 1984). The Los Angeles County Department of Public Social Services had been providing some homeless who qualified with emergency housing checks of $8.00, but a UCLA study of the motel/hotel market revealed that there is absolutely no housing available for that price (Heskin, 1984).

In most cities the private and public sectors fail to provide the services needed by thousands of homeless citizens. In some cases, as in Los Angeles, there is evidence that the existing social welfare "safety net" is intentionally filled with holes, to save money and discourage people from attempting to utilize public welfare—these holes actually cause hundreds of people in Los Angeles to become homeless every day.

National studies regarding who the new urban homeless are, where they came from, and where they may be going suggest that the homeless of the 1980s are the economic and social fallout of a social system riddled with contradictions and crises. These are people who have fallen through the cracks of a social structure that is being profoundly shaken and reshaped by long-term economic and social trends and current political policies. The causes of homelessness in the 1980s are not to be found primarily in individual pathology, such as personal instability, drug and alcohol dependence, mental illness, or a lack of "marketable" job skills or "correct" social attitudes, but in the social, economic, and political processes that are transforming our society. As Governor Mario Cuomo of New York State has put it,

> The nature of our homeless population is largely misunderstood.
>
> The lives of most of them are like the lives of the people we all know in our families, in our own communities. They are homeless because they are unemployed, because of chronic poverty, or simply because of the nationwide shortage of affordable housing (quoted in Riordan, 1987, p. 27).

It is the intention of this book to demonstrate that contemporary homelessness is essentially the effect of increasing social and economic inequality upon those in our society who are most vulnerable to individual, family, and economic instability.

Despite the magnitude and scope of the problem, most of the existing published literature on the homeless is descriptive and dominated by psychological/psychiatric interpretations. This book includes, but goes beyond, psychology and psychiatry, to bring together the insights of history, sociology, political science, and epidemiology in a comprehensive framework for understanding the issue. It is essentially a case study of the Los Angeles homeless population, one of the largest in the nation, and its conditions. The case study is presented against the backdrop of history and the national homelessness crisis. The perspective taken is sociological; consequently, those without homes are identified and understood as a segment of the social stratification system of the United States. No explanation of the homelessness crisis can be adequate without placing the homeless in the larger scheme of our socioeconomic structure. The reality of homelessness, which too many Americans live every day, should not be isolated from the dynamics of the social system in which they live.

In addition to an original empirical analysis of the homeless issue, the reader will be provided with a historical account of homelessness since the end of the Civil War and an examination of the historical and social structural factors believed to have given rise to the new urban homelessness of the 1980s. The following developments are analyzed in terms of their contribution to the rise of the contemporary problem of homelessness:

the low-income housing crisis,
deindustrialization,
recession and record-level unemployment,
increases in the poverty rate,
cutbacks in social welfare programs,
increasing family instability and domestic violence,
deinstitutionalization of the mentally ill, and
the policies of the Reagan Administration.

A sociological model using the concepts of disaffiliation and displacement is offered to explain homelessness theoretically, and a typology of the homeless is developed. Both model and typology attempt to link the psychological, social, cultural, and economic dimensions of homelessness together to provide a theoretical and analytic approach to understanding homelessness.

Triangulation shapes the overall research design of this book. Three well-established sociological methods were utilized to arrive at the findings and conclusions. The first was survey research. The second involved qualitative data as manifested in the biographical declarations of homeless persons, legal declarations of professionals who work with the homeless, and court records of several landmark legal suits filed on behalf of the homeless in Los Angeles. The third is the author's personal observation of various aspects of homelessness, which brings special sensitivity to an appreciation of the quantitative and qualitative data.

Two empirical research studies conducted in Los Angeles County and the research findings of studies conducted in major cities and by various government agencies provide the quantitative empirical basis for this book.

The survey data base of the book is unique in a number of ways. All the original data were collected in 1984 in Los Angeles County.

The first data set is a sample of 269 homeless men and women from six sites in Los Angeles County. These data were collected by the Basic Shelter Research Project, Psychiatric Epidemiology Program, UCLA, under the direction of the author. What is significant about this sample compared to samples from other cities is the comprehensiveness of the information obtained. A questionnaire containing over 200 items, requiring, on the average, a one-hour interview, was used to gain in-depth information on the following characteristics of homeless persons:

basic demographics,

welfare status and use,

economic and employment history and status,

homelessness history and status,

physical health status and care utilization,

mental health status and care utilization,

drug and alcohol use, and

crime victimization.

A second detailed random sample of 174 skid row SRO residents was obtained by the author while directing an analysis of a study for the Community Redevelopment Agency of the City of Los Angeles. SRO residents are what many social scientists refer to as the traditional homeless or borderline homeless.

Also reviewed are various public and private sector proposals to aid the homeless. An examination of the politics of homelessness is presented, focusing on attempts by the homeless themselves to organize politically, is also discussed. The Reagan Administration's response to the problem is also discussed. Major legal strategies to aid the homeless in Los Angeles are reviewed and evaluated.

A critical analysis of psychiatric explanations of homelessness is offered. In place of psychiatric explanations, an alternative social structural position is taken. An understanding of social stratification and its consequences for human behavior and consciousness is pivotal to a sociological perspective. The status of an individual within a social class is one of the most important explanatory approaches in social science (Szymanski, 1983, p. 1). The behavior and mental state of a class of individuals cannot be adequately understood without knowing how they come to be positioned in their particular segment of the stratification system.

Finally, the implications of the empirical data, the response of the public and private sectors to the homelessness problem, and the concerns and ideas of the homeless themselves will be assessed with an eye toward suggesting the direction responsive social policy should take to address the problem of homelessness.

Chapter 1

THE NEW URBAN HOMELESS

An Empirical Profile

On any given night there are at least 250,000 residents of the United States who are homeless (HUD 1984) and each year as many as 3 million who experience some type of homelessness (Hopper & Hamberg, 1986). A growing body of data from research conducted in major cities and states across the United States (Los Angeles, San Francisco, Portland, Dallas, Phoenix, St. Louis, Chicago, New York City, Ohio, and Utah; see Table 1.1) indicates that, compared with previous generations of the skid row homeless, the new homeless of the 1980s are younger, better educated, and disproportionately nonwhite.

In the recent past, social scientists described and explained the imminent disappearance of skid rows and skid row populations (Lee 1980; Bogue 1963). However, in many cities today, the "skid row" way of life no longer appears to be confined to a particular geographical area; it is overflowing, and has become a way of life throughout our cities' streets.

While a large literature exists on the skid row homeless of the past, there are few published comprehensive empirical studies of the problems and conditions of the contemporary urban homeless. This chapter reviews empirical profiles of

TABLE 1.1
Comparison of Homeless Population Samples from Select Cities and States (in Percentages)

Characteristic	City of Los Angeles Total	Male	Female	City of San Francisco Total	City of Portland Total	State of Utah Total	City of Dallas Total	City of Phoenix Total	City of Chicago Total	State of Ohio Total	City of New York Total	Male	Female
Age													
40 or younger	63	64	65	48	60	—	—	61	43[b]	62	66	67	64
60 or older	6	6	6	19	7	—	—	3	8[c]	6	5	5	8
Mean	37	38	35	—	38	34	(33)[a]	37	—	—	—	36	36
Gender													
Male	78	—	—	96	85	79	88	86	67	81	78	—	—
Female	22	—	—	4	15	21	12	14	33	19	22	—	—
Race													
White	49	49	50	52	77	84	53	64	67	65	14	14	25
Black	32	34	36	26	6	3	7	9	33	30	64	64	56
Hispanic	10	10	14	14	4	3	3	17	1	4	18	18	9
Native American	6	4	10	3	10	6	—	9	2	—	—	—	—
Other	3	3	—	5	1	4	—	1	—	1	4	4	—
Education													
Completed high school	64	66	56	56	47	12 years (average)	34	60	—	31	—	45	54
Some postsecondary education	38	39	33	25	24		18	34	—	14	—	17	24
Marital status													
Never married	54	57	40	74	40	—	44	46	—	45	—	—	—
Married	6	6	9	4	12	—	12	13	—	9	—	—	—
Divorced/separated	36	35	40	17	36	—	40	37	—	39	—	—	—
Widowed	4	2	11	4	5	—	4	4	—	5	—	—	—

Employment status												
Employed full or part time	20	20	23	18	8	21	—	16	29	25	4	4
Unemployed and looking	50	50	44	—	—	76	—	—	—	47	44	28
Unemployed and not looking (includes retired and disabled)	30	30	33	—	—	—	—	—	—	—	—	—
Income												
None	25	21	24	—	13	32	—	8	15	36	—	—
Employment	19	17	24	—	21	45	—	16	29	27	—	—
Social Security	12	12	13	—	6	0	—	—	—	20	6	16
General welfare	13	11	22	—	12	10	—	11	50	38	6	12
Veterans Administration	4	5	2	—	—	0	—	—	10	—	—	—
Blood bank	5	6	—	—	17	—	—	12	—	2	—	—
Veteran												
Yes	36	45	5	47	46	—	—	46	—	32	28	—
Vietnam (percentage of veterans)	18	30	—	—	—	—	—	36	—	9	—	—
Receiving public assistance	29	27	31	—	—	16	—	24	28	45	—	—
History of psychiatric hospitalization	19	17	26	9	17	—	13	17	23	29	15	28

Sources: City of Los Angeles, from R. Ropers, The contribution of economic and political policies and trends to the rise of the new urban homeless, in US Congress, House, Committee on Government Operations, Internal Relations and Human Resources Subcommittee, *The Federal Response to the Homeless Crisis*, (Washington, DC: the Committee, 1985), pp. 833–856, and The rise of the new urban homeless, *Public Affairs Report* (Institute of Governmental Studies, University of California at Berkeley) 26 (5&6). Sample size 269: 211 males, 58 females).

City of San Francisco, from M. Navarro, Homeless program passes test in rain, *San Francisco Examiner*, October 17, 1984, p. B5. Sample size unknown.

City of Portland, from R. Caulk, *The homeless poor: Multnomah County* (Portland, OR: Social Services Div., 1983). Sample size 131.

State of Utah, from L. Russell and J. Maurin, *Survey of Utah's homeless: Preliminary report* (Salt Lake City: Mayor's Task Force for the Appropriate Treatment for the Mentally Ill, 1986), sample size 243; *Homelessness in Utah: Problems and recommendations, A guide for policymakers and providers* (Salt Lake City: Mayor's Task Force, 1986).

City of Dallas, from G. Lumsden, *Issues associated with housing the indigent: The Salvation Army set-up shelter program* (Dallas: Department of Health and Human Services, 1983). Sample size 104.

City of Phoenix, from C. Brown, et al., *Homeless of Phoenix: Who are they? And what should be done?* (Phoenix: Phoenix South Community Health Center, 1983). Sample size 195.

City of Chicago, from *Homelessness in Chicago* (Chicago: City of Chicago, Department of Human Services, Social Services Task Force, 1983). Sample size 82.

State of Ohio, from *Homelessness in Ohio: A study of people in need* (Ohio Department of Mental Health, Office of Program Evaluation and Research, 1985). Sample size 979.

City of New York, S. Crystal and M. Goldstein, *The homeless in New York City shelters* (New York: City of New York, Human Resources Administration, 1984). Sample size 7,884: 6,121 males, 1,763 females.

[a] Median
[b] ≤ age 35
[c] ≥ age 55

Note: Data from all these studies were collected using survey research interviews. Not all of the studies collected the same kinds of data; consequently, some studies lack information on certain variables.

the homeless populations in select cities and states across the country. An in-depth profile and analysis of the characteristics of the homeless of Los Angeles County is presented as a case study of the new urban homeless.

In 1984 the U.S. Department of Housing and Urban Development (HUD) designated the homeless population of Los Angeles County one of the largest (33,800) in the nation. The homeless are distributed throughout the county but are concentrated in two major clusters, specifically in the downtown skid row area, also referred to as L.A. Central City East and the Westside (Venice and Santa Monica).

NATIONAL PROFILE

Because of the growing need to assess and deal with the problem, several profiles of the homeless in major cities and some states have emerged in the last few years. Regional differences undoubtedly affect the makeup of homeless populations, and there are also differences in survey methodologies, but it is possible to make comparisons on a number of key demographic variables.

There are striking similarities in the profiles of the homeless in samples across the country. As a group, the new urban homeless are younger than earlier "skid row" homeless populations, which were dominated by individuals in their fifties and sixties; the current average age of the homeless population is between thirty-six and thirty-eight years. (See Table 1.1.) According to the HUD report, 65 percent of the homeless are in their late twenties to mid-thirties.

Women are still a minority among the homeless, representing about 20 percent of that population, although in the past they may have constituted only about 5 percent of the homeless. Racial composition is another revealing demographic characteristic of the new homeless: blacks, Hispanics, and Native Americans are overrepresented. While there is regional variation, roughly half of the homeless populations in most areas are members of minority groups. This is a major change; 20 years ago at least 90 percent of the skid row homeless populations were white. In New York City, 86 percent of the shelter population are nonwhite; in Los Angeles, 51%; and in Dallas, 47%. (See Table 1.1.) Homeless blacks constitute the largest and most overrepresented minority group. While nonwhites make up only a small percentage (16 percent) of the homeless population in a state like Utah, they are nonetheless disproportionately represented in the homeless population in relation to their numbers in the general Utah population (5 percent).

Many homeless persons have at least a high school education, and depending on the region, between 20 and 40 percent have some education beyond high school.

Although stereotypes of the homeless as bums and hobos still abound, the available evidence suggests that many homeless persons are unemployed but actively looking for work. Some of them, the working homeless, are employed full time or part time. Such working homeless constitute 20 percent of the homeless population in Los Angeles, 29 percent in Chicago, 25 percent in Ohio, and 21 percent in Utah. In New York City, 44 percent of the homeless males are looking for work, and in Los Angeles 50 percent are looking for work.

From one-third to almost one-half of homeless males are veterans. In cities that report the information, about one-third of the homeless vets are Vietnam veterans (Los Angeles, 30 percent; Phoenix, 36 percent).

In city after city only a minority of the homeless have been in psychiatric hospitals (Los Angeles, 19 percent; Portland, 17 percent; Dallas, 13 percent; Phoenix, 17 percent; Chicago, 23 percent; New York City, 20 percent).

Many have been without homes for less than a year; this was true of 64 percent in Los Angeles. The HUD report concluded, "While there is a sizable minority of chronically homeless persons, most of the homeless have been so for a fairly short period of time" (1984, p. 29).

THE HOMELESS OF LOS ANGELES: A CASE STUDY

In the 1980s, California has been estimated to have as many as 90,000 homeless residents (Waters, 1984, p. 2). This is not the first time California has been host to a large homeless population—in 1931 a committee from the Chamber of Commerce of Los Angeles petitioned the governor of California to call out the National Guard to keep the "horde" of homeless at the state's borders out (Cross & Cross, 1937, p. 4). It was estimated in 1933 that by "midwinter peak" the homeless population of California numbered 125,000 (Cross & Cross, 1937, p. 43).

This section examines data from 269 comprehensive interviews of homeless men and women. A description is offered of the population studied in terms of its demographic and homeless history characteristics, minority group status, health status, various mental health indicators, and health service utilization of homeless persons.

Since no physical examination could be conducted during the interview, a self-reported index of health status, or perceived health status, was used as a proxy indicator of global mental, social, and physical health. The value of self-reported health status has been demonstrated to be a means of summarizing objective and subjective aspects of health (Fillenbaum, 1979, p. 45; Singer, Garfinkel, & Cohen, 1976, p. 517). A test of the construct validity of such a general health index when used among a homeless population is also included. Multiple regression is utilized to identify health correlates of perceived health status. If the index is a valid measure of general health, it should be substantially related to other measures of physical and mental health and to health and illness behaviors. Subsequent to this test of the construct validity of perceived health status among the homeless, multiple regression is used to look at the contribution of demographic and homeless history variables to the homeless individuals' health status.

Methodology

The sampling strategy used was *cluster sampling*. When a complete list of a population is unavailable, as is the case with a homeless population, cluster sampling "takes advantage of the geographical concentration of portions of the population and does not require a complete list of the population" (Eckhardt & Ermann, 1977, p. 203).

Major geographical concentrations of homeless persons

were identified in Los Angeles County by a committee of experts, members of the Basic Shelter Working Group organized by the Legal Aid Foundation of Los Angeles. Two major clusters of homeless individuals in Los Angeles County were identified, in the downtown Los Angeles skid row and the Westside (Santa Monica and Venice).

Within each of these two major clusters, three large subclusters of homeless individuals were identified. Within the downtown cluster, the largest shelter in Los Angeles (600 homeless individuals can be accommodated), the soup kitchen line, and the only shelter for homeless women were identified as major subclusters. In the Westside cluster, the three subclusters that were identified were the main shelter in Santa Monica, the largest soup kitchen line in Venice, and a well-known "hangout" parking lot.

Systematic sampling techniques (every third person) were used at the downtown shelter and soup kitchen and at the Westside soup kitchen (76 percent of the respondents). As Babbie has pointed out, "In practice, systematic sampling is virtually identical to simple random sampling. By now, debates over the relative merits of simple random sampling and systematic sampling have been resolved largely in favor of the simpler method: systematic sampling" (Babbie, 1975, p. 155). In the remaining subclusters an attempt was made to interview total populations.

The uniqueness of the total sample is that, unlike other studies of the homeless in Los Angeles (Farr, Koegel, & Burnam, 1986), it is not restricted to the downtown skid row area and it includes a sample of homeless women.

Many different subgroups of the homeless are included in the total sample; for example, individuals who had spent the previous night sleeping in the streets (20 percent), on the beach (2 percent), in vehicles (9 percent), in shelters (47 percent), in single room occupancy (SRO) hotels (17 percent), and at the apartments of friends or relatives (5 percent).

The criterion for inclusion in the samples was lack of a stable residence of one's own, that is, a place to sleep and receive mail that is not dependent on such sources as welfare, charity, or friendship.

A total of 509 persons were contacted, and 269 agreed to

be interviewed—a response rate of 52.3 percent. No monetary or other incentives were used. Comparisons of interviewers' ratings of appearance, age, gender, race, and behavioral characteristics of nonrespondents and respondents from two sites ($n = 199$), show no significant differences. Previous empirical studies have verified the reliability of self-reported answers given by homeless persons (Bahr & Houts, 1971, p. 374; Robertson, Ropers, & Boyer, 1985).

The interviews were conducted using the Basic Shelter Interview Schedule (BSI). The BSI contains 200 questions subdivided into eight sections: demographic characteristics, welfare status, economic and employment history, homelessness history, physical and mental health status, health service utilization, alcohol use patterns, and crime victimization.

Many of the BSI questions have been adapted from other health surveys. Some of the demographic, alcohol-use patterns, and psychiatric assessment items were adapted from the National Institute of Mental Health (NIMH) Diagnostic Interview Schedule (DIS). Most of the health status and health service utilization questions were taken from the Los Angeles Health Survey questionnaire. Depressive symptoms were assessed using the Center for Epidemiological Studies Depression Scale (CES-D). The level of alcoholism was assessed using a modified version of the alcoholism scale of the Diagnostic Interview Schedule. Based on the pattern of alcohol use and level of impairment in social and occupational functioning, a respondent was assigned to one of three categories: asymptomatic, alcohol abusing, or alcohol dependent. The BSI was pretested with 20 homeless persons from the skid row area. Interviews were conducted by 28 trained volunteers over a six-month period between December 1983 and May 1984.

Results

Table 1.2 presents demographic characteristics of the sample. More than three-quarters (78.4 percent) of the sample was male. The respondents' ages ranged from 17 to 76; the mean age was 37.5 years. One-half of the respondents were nonwhite (50.6 percent). Blacks constituted the largest minority

TABLE 1.2
Sample Characteristics

Characteristic	(n)	Percentage	Mean
Gender			
Female	(58)	21.6	—
Male	(211)	78.4	—
Age	(269)	—	37.45
Ethnicity			
White	(133)	49.4	—
Nonwhite	(136)	50.6	—
Marital status			
Have been married	(123)	46.1	—
Never been married	(136)	53.5	—
Education			
8th grade or less	(32)	11.9	—
Some high school	(65)	24.3	—
High school diploma	(70)	26.1	—
Other beyond high school	(23)	8.6	—
Some college or more	(78)	29.1	—
Veteran[a]	(88)	45.4	—
Vietnam Veteran[a]	(16)	29.6	—
Monthly Income for 1984	(269)	—	261.01
Employment Status			
Full-time employed	(15)	5.8	—
Part-time employed	(37)	14.2	—
Looking for a job	(127)	48.5	—
Not looking	(57)	21.9	—
Retired, disabled, or other	(44)	9.2	—
Unemployment (weeks)[b]	(236)	—	252.66
Months since last full-time job[b]	(236)	—	43.68

[a] Males only.
[b] Respondents not retired, disabled, or other.

group (32.3 percent), followed by Hispanics (10.4 percent), Native Americans (4.8 percent), Asians (0.7 percent), and others (2.2 percent). More than one-half of the sample (53.0 percent) reported having never been married, and nearly all (93.6 percent) were not currently married. Six of ten respondents (63.8 percent) indicated that they had completed high school or gone beyond. Of the males, 45 percent were veterans and 29.6 percent were Vietnam veterans.

When questioned about their income, almost three-quarters (70.6 percent) reported a usual monthly income of $300.00 or less. The mean monthly income was $261.00, whereas the median was $150.00. Employment was the principle source of income for 20 percent of the sample. About one-third (28.5 percent) received some sort of transfer payment: Social Security (30.0 percent), county welfare (42.0 percent), or veterans' benefits (3.3 percent). More than one-third of the sample reported no income at the time of the interview.

The large majority of the sample was part of the labor force: 14.2 percent worked part time; 5.8 percent worked full time; and 48.5 percent indicated that they were looking for work. One-fifth of the sample (21.9 percent) was unemployed and not looking for work, others (9.2 percent) were retired or disabled and thus not looking for employment. Excluding the disabled, retired, and other persons with unspecified employment status, the homeless individuals interviewed were without work for an average of 253 weeks (median = 111 weeks) and without a full-time job for an average of 44 months (median = 24 months). As a group, the nonwhite homeless had been unemployed longer (mean = 9.9 months) than the homeless whites (mean = 8.6 months; $t = 2.49$, $P < 0.01$).[*]

Selected homelessness characteristics of the population are presented in Table 1.3. The mean number of weeks without a place of one's own to live was 74.4 weeks. The majority of respondents (74.0 percent) reported having been homeless for

---

[*]The t test compares differences between mean scores; P is probability.

TABLE 1.3
Homelessness History

Characteristic	(n)	Percentage	Mean
Weeks with no place	(269)	—	74.4
Reasons for homelessness			
No money	(94)	51.9	—
No job	(65)	35.9	—
No welfare	(6)	3.3	—
Family crisis	(4)	2.2	—
Psychological problem	(2)	1.1	—
State of the economy	(1)	0.6	—
Drug or alcohol abuse	(1)	0.6	—
Other	(8)	4.4	—
Number of times moved during the last year	(207)	—	9.9
Days in shelter in the last 30 days	(269)	—	10.9
Length of residency in Los Angeles (months)	(269)	—	68.0
Availability of someone to "hang out" with	(250)	30.4	—
Receive public assistance			
Yes	(76)	28.5	—
No	(191)	71.5	—
When you eat, where do you usually get food?			
Soup kitchen/pantry	(58)	25.8	—
Mission/shelter	(121)	53.8	—
Market	(16)	7.1	—
Cafe/restaurant	(19)	8.4	—
Friend	(5)	2.2	—
Garbage	(1)	0.4	—
Other	(5)	2.2	—
Meals per day			
1 meal	(10)	9.5	—
2 meals	(35)	33.3	2.49
3 meals	(59)	56.2	—
4 meals	(1)	1.0	—
Victim of a crime	(87)	33.9	—

one year or less, and almost one-third (32 percent) had been homeless for one month or less. The most frequent reasons given by the respondents for their homelessness related to their financial situations (91.7 percent), including: lack of money, unemployment, the state of the economy, and lack of welfare support. The homeless interviewed had moved an average of ten times during the preceding year (median = 2). In the preceding month, the sample had stayed an average of 10.9 nights in missions or shelters. Although a large part of the sample (46.5 percent) had not stayed overnight in a shelter during the previous 30 days, more than half (51.2 percent) had spent the previous night in a shelter. The mean length of residency in Los Angeles County was 68 weeks, and the majority of the respondents (76 percent) had stayed in the area for two years or more. A third of the sample (30.4 percent) indicated they had "someone to hang out with." Most (72 percent) receive no public assistance. Eating at soup kitchens or shelters is common (79.6 percent) among the sample. Among those who answered the question, only little more than half (56 percent) indicated that they eat three meals a day. Almost 34 percent of the respondents had been victims of a crime in the six months preceding the interview.

Table 1.4 presents data on acute and chronic health problems, use of health services, health insurance, and medical coverage. The distribution of this population on the index of perceived health is also included in this table.

Of the sample, 66.6 percent rated their overall health as either good or excellent; 21.2 percent rated their health as fair; and 12.2 percent considered themselves to be in poor health. More than four persons out of ten (45.7 percent) reported that their health had deteriorated since they became homeless; nevertheless, 38 percent indicated no change and 16.3 percent considered their health improved. Almost 40 percent reported that they had been victims of an accident or of an acute illness within the last two months. Among the accidents ($n = 23$), broken bones were the most frequent (30.4 percent), followed by cuts (26.1 percent). Falls and burns accounted for a smaller proportion of accidents (13 and 4.3 percent respectively). The most prevalent self-reported acute health problems ($n = 71$)

TABLE 1.4
Homeless Health Status

Characteristic	(n)	Percentage
Perceived health status		
Poor	(31)	12.2
Fair	(54)	21.2
Good	(98)	38.4
Excellent	(72)	28.2
Perceived health since homeless (n = 87)		
Worse	(42)	45.7
Same	(15)	38.0
Better	(35)	16.3
Sickness or accident in the previous two months		
No accident or illness	(152)	60.6
Accident or illness	(99)	39.4
Type of acute health problem		
Accidents (n = 23)		
Broken bones	(7)	30.4
Cuts	(6)	26.1
Falls	(3)	13.0
Burns	(1)	4.3
Other accidents	(6)	26.1
Acute illness (n = 71)		
Flu, cold, bronchitis	(26)	36.6
Ankle, feet or legs	(7)	9.9
Headache, backache	(7)	9.9
High blood pressure [sic]	(4)	5.6
Other	(27)	38.0
Stayed in bed for accident or acute illness	(40)	16.9
Contacted health professional for accident or acute illness	(50)	55.6
Source of medical attention for accident or acute illness		
Free or shelter clinic	(16)	34.8
County hospital or clinic	(15)	32.6
Community hospital	(7)	15.2

TABLE 1.4 (*continued*)

Characteristic	(*n*)	Percentage
Veterans hospital	(4)	8.7
Private physician or other	(4)	8.7
Chronic illness	(99)	39.8
Type of chronic health problem (*n* = 70)		
High blood pressure	(27)	38.6
Arthritis	(9)	12.9
Bronchitis/cough	(8)	11.4
Asthma	(6)	8.6
Diabetes	(5)	7.1
Cancer	(4)	5.7
Epilepsy	(3)	4.3
Heart condition	(2)	2.9
Other	(6)	8.6
Recentness of medical consultation re: chronic health problem		
12 months or less	(45)	51.7
More than 12 months	(30)	34.5
Never	(12)	13.8
Hospitalization in past 12 months for any condition	(25)	29.8
Feelings of depression in past year	(171)	71.0
Alcoholism symptomatology		
Asymptomatic	(148)	55.0
Alcohol abusing	(70)	26.0
Alcohol dependent	(51)	19.0
Used drugs more than five times	(122)	53.7
Drugs used more than five times		
Marijuana[a]	(124)	86.1
Amphetamines[b]	(58)	47.9
Barbituates[c]	(49)	38.9
Tranquilizers[d]	(33)	29.2
Heroin	(22)	20.0
Cocaine	(46)	38.3

TABLE 1.4 (*continued*)

Opiates[e]	(30)	26.8
Psychedelics[f]	(39)	34.5
Other		
Self-reported drug dependence	(43)	24.4
Lifetime hospitalization		
Emotional/nervous problem	(42)	15.6
Substance abuse problem	(34)	12.6
Both	(8)	3.0
CES-D*cases (*n* = 82)	(41)	50.0
No health insurance	(200)	78.4
Type of medical insurance		
Medical (Medicaid)	(22)	40.0
Private	(13)	23.6
Medicare	(13)	23.6
Veterans benefits	(6)	10.9
Other	(1)	1.8

[a] Includes hashish, pot, grass.
[b] Includes stimulants, uppers, speeds.
[c] Includes sedatives, downers, sleeping pills.
[d] Includes Valium and Librium.
[e] Other than heroin (demerol, codeine, morphine).
[f] LSD, mescaline, peyote, psilocybin, DMT.
* Center for Epidemiological Studies Depression Scale.

were in the category of influenza, colds, coughs, and bronchitis (36.6 percent). Almost 10 percent mentioned headaches and backaches, and another 9.9 percent indicated problems with their ankles, feet, or legs. Other kinds of acute health problems were reported by 38 percent. Of those who reported an accident or an illness in the past two months, 55.6 percent had contacted a health professional about this problem. The more frequent medical contacts were made at a free or shelter clinic (34.8 percent) or at the county hospital or clinic (32.6 percent); other facilities used included the community hospital (15.2 percent) and the veteran's hospital (8.7 percent). The reasons most frequently given for not contacting a health professional for acute health problems were that the respondents had not considered the problems serious enough (50 percent) and that they were unable to pay for medical services (21.2 percent).

Chronic physical health problems were reported by 39.8 percent. Among these, 38.6 percent ($n = 27$) reported high blood pressure. Other chronic problems were arthritis (12.9 percent), bronchitis or emphysema (11.4 percent), asthma (8.6 percent), diabetes (7.1 percent), cancer (5.7 percent), epilepsy (4.3 percent), and heart conditions (2.9 percent).

More than half of those reporting a chronic condition (51.7 percent) indicated that they had seen a physician for this condition in the last 12 months. Another one-third (34.5 percent) had consulted a health professional more than one year before the interview, whereas 13.8 percent had never seen a doctor for their chronic conditions. The most common reasons given for not consulting for a chronic condition were that the problem was not serious enough (30.4 percent), that it could not be treated (26.1 percent), and that the respondent did not have enough money (10.9 percent). Among those reporting a chronic condition, 29.8 percent indicated that they had been hospitalized in the past 12 months. Among those hospitalized, 52 percent reported one hospitalization and 48 percent indicated two or more. The average length of these hospitalizations was six days.

A majority of respondents (71.0 percent) reported having felt sad, blue, or depressed during the previous 12 months. The mean duration of these depressive states had been 11 weeks. The most frequent reasons evoked for depression were not having a job or enough money (30.4 percent) and separation from family (13.1 percent). When probed about their alcohol use, 64 percent indicated that they did sometimes have beer, wine, or other alcoholic beverages. From the information on lifetime experience with alcohol of all the respondents, 55 percent are categorized as asymptomatic, 26 percent are classified as alcohol abusers, and 19 percent had reached the alcohol dependence level. When asked about lifetime experience with various drugs, slightly more than half (53.7 percent) reported using nonprescription drugs more than five times in their life. Marijuana was the drug that had been used most often by this group (86 percent). While drug use is not uncommon, only a minority (24.4 percent) indicated they were drug dependent. Multiple substance abusers (alcohol and other drugs) constitute 19 percent of the respondents. Furthermore, the lifetime prevalence of hospitalization for emotional or substance abuse disorders is 31.2 percent, with 15.6 percent indicating hospitalization for emotional or nervous problems and 12.6 percent reporting hospitalization for alcohol or drug problems; 3 percent had been hospitalized for both conditions.

The CES-D was administered to a subsample from the skid row area ($n = 82$). The mean CES-D score for the sample is 18 (median = 15.5). Using the standard cutting point of 16 to identify a probable case of depression for the current week, 50 percent of the individuals responding could be classed as depressed (Roberts & Vernon, 1983).

Respondents were also questioned on their medical coverage. A large majority (78.4 percent) indicated no health insurance. Of those who reported having medical coverage, 40 percent were covered by Medical (Medicaid), 23.6 percent by Medicare, and 23.6 percent by private insurance, while 10.9 percent received veterans benefits.

Gender Differences

Of the homeless sampled in Los Angeles, 77 percent were men and 23 percent were women. (Other cities report that women comprise from 12 percent to 30 percent of their homeless.) The homeless women in Los Angeles did not differ significantly from the men in regard to age, race, or education, but the women were more likely to have been married previously, and there were significantly greater proportions of women who were divorced, separated, or widowed. (See Table 1.5.)

In the Los Angeles sample, however, the women on the average had been homeless for shorter periods of time than men. Over three-fourths (78 percent) had been homeless less than 12 months, compared to 60 percent of the men. The leading reasons given for their homelessness among both men and women were: no money/no job (87.8 percent).

The health of homeless women also differed significantly

TABLE 1.5

Select Differences between Homeless Men and Homeless Women

Characteristic	Percentage			Chi-square Probability (χ^2)
	Total	Male	Female	
Marital status				
Never married	54	57	40	
Married	6	6	9	
Divorced/separated	36	35	40	
Widowed	4	2	11	≤.05
	(n = 267)	(n = 210)	(n = 57)	
Duration of homelessness				
12 months or less	64	60	78	
More than 12 months	34	40	22	≤.01
	(n = 196)	(n = 146)	(n = 50)	

Self-rated health status			
Excellent/good	67	71	52
Fair/poor	33	29	48
	(n = 255)	(n = 200)	(n = 55) ≤.05
Sickness or accident in last two months			
Yes	39	36	54
No	61	64	46
	(n = 251)	(n = 199)	(n = 52) ≤.05
Chronic or recurring illness			
Yes	40	33	65
No	60	67	35
	(n = 249)	(n = 198)	(n = 51) ≤.01

NOTE: Chi-square (χ^2) is a frequently-used test of statistical significance to demonstrate that observed differences in values do not occur by chance. A probability of ≤ (less than or equal to) .05 indicates that the observed difference in values had a 5 percent or less possibility of occurring by chance.

from that of men. A higher proportion of women reported their health status as fair or poor, a higher proportion had been sick or had had an accident in the previous two months. Much higher proportions of women also reported having a chronic or recurring illness. (See Table 1.5.) Since they had become homeless, 42 percent of the men and 31 percent of the women reported their health was worse. Although only 19 percent of the sample reported that they had been previously hospitalized for psychiatric reasons, a higher proportion of women (26 percent) than men (17 percent) reported psychiatric hospitalization. This difference is not, however, statistically significant.

Multivariate Analysis

In order to determine the construct validity of perceived health status among homeless individuals and to identify demographic and homeless history correlates of health status, stepwise multiple regressions were used. Evaluation of the assumptions for the regressions led to the transformation of some variables to reduce the skewness of their distribution and improve the normality, linearity, and homoscedasticity of residuals. Logarithmic transformations were used on the length of unemployment and income. Considering the exploratory nature of these analyses, the level of significance adopted for change in R^2 is 0.10.[*]

To test the validity of perceived health as measured among the homeless, a first stepwise multiple regression indicates that four health variables contribute significantly to the explanation of perceived health status. After the elimination of nonsignificant variables, another stepwise regression was run. Table 1.6 presents the results of this analysis. It displays the standardized regression coefficient (BETA), the increment in R^2 produced by each variable, and the level of significance for change in R^2 induced by the inclusion of each variable in the equation.

---

[*]R^2 is variance explained.

TABLE 1.6
Stepwise Multiple Regression of Perceived Health
(n = 208)

Predictor[a]	BETA[b]	Change in R^2	p
Chronic condition (no = 1, yes = 2)	0.33	0.17	<0.001
Contact doctor for acute condition (no = 1, yes = 2)	0.21	0.04	<0.001
Weeks sad or depressed	0.14	0.03	<0.002
Alcoholism symptomatology (asymptomatic = 1, abuser = 2, alcohol dependent = 3)	0.14	0.02	<0.01
Total R^2		0.26	

Excellent = 1; good = 2; fair = 3; poor = 4.
[a] Other variables in the model: stayed in bed for the past 2 months for illness or injuries, number of days in bed, hospitalized for substance abuse, hospitalized for emotional problem, ever had visual hallucination, ever had auditory hallucination, sick or accident in the past 2 months, hospitalized in the past 12 months.
[b] Standardized regression coefficient.

Being afflicted by a chronic condition is the best correlate of perceived health (change in R^2 = 0.17, p<0.001). Consultation of a physician for an acute condition (change in R^2 = 0.04, p<0.001), duration of depressed mood (change in R^2 = 0.03, p<0.002), and alcoholism symptomatology (change in R^2 = 0.02, p<0.01) are also significant correlates of perceived health in this population. Overall, these four variables explain 26 percent of the variance observed in perceived health status. In summary, homeless persons with a chronic condition, having contacted a physician for an acute health problem, being in a depressed mood for a long period, and presenting severe alcoholism symptoms are the ones who are most likely to have perceived their health as poor. The same analysis was conducted on the subsample that was administered the CES-D scale. The CES-D score was the strongest predictor of perceived health status (change in R^2 = 0.24, p<0.001), followed by affliction with a chronic condition (change in R^2 = 0.10, p<0.01).

A stepwise multiple regression analysis was also used to look at the multivariate associations of demographic and homelessness history variables with perceived health status. Thirteen variables were considered simultaneously. As indicated in Table 1.7, the number of weeks unemployed (change in $R^2 = 0.03$, $p<0.01$) and education (change in $R^2 = 0.03$, $p<0.01$) are the best predictors of health status. Furthermore, gender (change in $R^2 = 0.01$, $p<0.10$), the number of nights spent in shelters or missions (change in $R^2 = 0.02$, $p<0.05$), the respondent's age (change in $R^2 = 0.01$, $p<0.05$), monthly income (change in $R^2 = 0.01$, $p<0.10$), and whether the respondent had been a victim of a crime in the previous six months (change in $R^2 = 0.01$, $p<0.10$) are also significant correlates of perceived health status. These seven variables explained 12 percent of the variance observed in perceived health status.

TABLE 1.7
Stepwise Multiple Regression of Perceived Health
in Relation to Demographic and Homelessness History Variables
($n = 249$)

Predictor[a]	BETA[b]	Change in R^2	p
Log week (+1) since unemployed	0.15	0.03	<0.01
Education (grade school = 1, . . . college = 5)	−0.15	0.03	<0.01
Gender (female = 1, male = 2)	−0.15	0.01	<0.10
Night in shelter or mission	−0.15	0.02	<0.05
Age	0.13	0.01	<0.05
Log monthly income (+1) for 1984	−0.12	0.01	<0.10
Victim of a crime (no = 1, yes = 2)	0.11	0.01	<0.10
Total R^2		0.12	

Excellent = 1; good = 2; fair = 3; poor = 4.
[a] Other variables in the model: veteran, marital status, number of times moved in past year, ethnicity, having someone to hang out with, number of weeks with no place of one's own.
[b] Standardized regression coefficient.

Discussion

This sample of homeless men and women provides the basis for a case study of the demographic characteristics and health status of homeless individuals in Los Angeles.

The 1984 HUD study of the homeless in the United States concluded that "the demographic characteristics of the homeless have changed markedly over the last 30 years." The HUD study found the national mean age of the homeless to be 34 years; the mean age of the Los Angeles sample was 37.5 years.

Traditionally, homeless populations have been disproportionately male, and this appears to hold up in the Los Angeles sample, where the proportion of males is 78.4 percent. Many of the homeless men in the present samples were found to be veterans (45.4 percent), and of these, 29.6 percent claimed to be veterans of Vietnam. This finding is also similar to the findings of studies in Portland, Phoenix, and New York. However, there is some evidence that the homeless populations of past decades also had high percentages of veterans (Bogue, 1963).

Of special interest, because it is contrary to popular stereotypes, is that 20 percent of these Los Angeles homeless worked full or part time and that 48 percent claim to be actively looking for work. The percentage of those working full or part time in Los Angeles is similar to the percentages found in San Francisco (18 percent), Phoenix (16 percent), Chicago (29 percent), Ohio (25 percent), and Utah (21 percent).

It is well documented that previous generations of homeless persons, in the 1950s, 1960s, and 1970s, were predominantly white males (Bogue, 1963; HUD, 1984). Blacks and Hispanics, while overrepresented among the poor, were underrepresented among the skid row homeless. However, the urban homeless population of the 1980s comprises larger percentages of nonwhite homeless persons than ever before. Half (50.6 percent) of the homeless sampled in Los Angeles were nonwhite, with blacks (32.3 percent) making up the largest nonwhite group. In Los Angeles County, proportionately, blacks are 2.6 times more present among the homeless compared to their representation in the general population (U.S. Department of Commerce 1982). In New York City, 86 percent of the homeless population were nonwhite. As the HUD study pointed out, "the minority population is overrepresented among the homeless, a significant change from 20 years ago" (1984).

Slightly more than one-half (53.5 percent) of the respondents had never been married. This finding is consistent with other studies of the contemporary homeless; however, the predominance of young single males among the homeless mirrors the fact that, among the general population, 73 percent of males between 20 and 24 years old are single ("Snapshot of a Changing America" 1985). The majority (64 percent) of homeless respondents had completed high school, a finding which is similar to the percentage of high school graduates among the population of Los Angeles County (70 percent). One-third of the respondents had some college education. The mean monthly income for the respondents in 1984 was $261.00, which results in a mean yearly income of $3,182.00; this is considerably lower than the Los Angeles County average income for 1980, which was $8,303.00 (Robertson, Ropers, & Boyer, 1985).

It is not surprising, given the recession-level unemployment rates of Los Angeles County in the early 1980s (9.5 percent as late as July 1984), that the average length of unemployment of the homeless respondents was 252 weeks. Economic reasons were the principal reason given (87.8 percent) for being homeless.

Studies regarding private- and public-sector emergency shelter in Los Angeles County have demonstrated that only a minority (10 percent) of the homeless in Los Angeles can find emergency shelter on any given night (Robertson, Ropers, & Boyer, 1985); this may explain why almost half (47 percent) of the respondents had not stayed overnight in a shelter during the previous 30 days. Contrary to the public stereotypes that most of the homeless in Los Angeles have come to Los Angeles recently from other cities or states, 76 percent of the respondents had lived in Los Angeles for two years or more.

Summarizing its review of the national homeless data, the HUD study concluded that for most people who become homeless, their condition is recent and likely to be temporary. This generalization is supported by this Los Angeles homeless population, in that a majority (74 percent) reported having been homeless less than a year (median = 13 weeks).

HEALTH STATUS

Until Brickner and collaborators described the medical aspects of homelessness, very little was known about the health status of homeless persons in the United States (Brickner et al., 1985). Their findings originated from data collected from homeless patients seen in a free clinic in New York City. In addition to major chronic health problems such as diabetes mellitus, hypertension, and drug and alcohol abuse, homeless persons seem to be at risk for infestations, peripheral vascular diseases, trauma, and pulmonary tuberculosis.

Notwithstanding this crucial information, the data suggest that only one-half of the homeless persons suffering from either acute or chronic health problems contacted any health professional for their condition. Even if many did not seek health care because they judged their condition not serious enough, a large segment of homeless individuals still escape current clinical observations.

Among those with acute health problems, influenza, colds, and bronchitis represent the most often reported problems (27.7 percent), the prevalence of which can be explained in part by the fact that most of the interviews were conducted in winter, when the night temperature in Los Angeles often drops between 10 and 15 degrees Celsius. McAdams et al., (1985), reported high prevalence of tuberculosis among a homeless population of New York City—thus it is possible that these self-reported respiratory infections are masking more serious health problems. The high proportion of trauma (24.5 percent) among the acute health problems reported parallels the prevalence among hospitalized homeless persons (Kelly, 1985).

In this study, the prevalence of trauma is partially accounted for by the level of victimization in this population ($r = 0.21$, $p<0.001$).

Almost 40% of the population reported one chronic health problem; the most prevalent chronic or recurring illness is hypertension. Almost 10 percent of the homeless respondents reported this condition, which correlates with ethnicity (Black = 1, but Other = 0; $r = 0.14$, $p<0.05$). However, the results of a hypertension screening program among the homeless (Kellog et al., 1985) reveal that approximately 30 percent of the population surveyed had a confirmed diagnosis of hypertension. The prevalence was much higher (60 percent) among older residents of SRO hotels. One-quarter of the persons diagnosed were unaware of their condition; we can thus suspect that the current survey underestimates the true prevalence of hypertension.

The data indicate that the Los Angeles homeless population has limited access to health care. Almost 80 percent reported no medical coverage. This contrasts sharply with the level of medical coverage in national estimates (Robertson & Cousineau, 1986). For those reporting some health insurance, the majority (63.6 percent) indicated they are covered by either Medicaid or Medicare, and only 23.6 percent reported any private insurance. Surprisingly, only 2 percent of the respondents reported coverage by veterans benefits, whereas more than 45 percent of the males interviewed are veterans. This suggests that many homeless persons are not aware of their rights or do not have access to some of the health facilities that should be available to them.

It was found that the lifetime prevalence of hospitalization for any psychiatric disorder was 31.2 percent. Alcohol and drug abuse accounted for approximately half of these hospitalizations. Based on interviews conducted with the DIS as part of the Epidemiologic Catchment Area program, Fischer and collaborators (1986) found that only a small proportion of homeless have a current major mental illness (schizophrenia, affective disorders, cognitive impairment). This suggests that the use of lifetime hospitalization data overestimates greatly the current prevalence of major mental problems in the homeless population.

Not surprisingly, the level of demoralization in this population is very high. Seven out of ten respondents indicated they had felt sad, blue, or depressed during the previous 12 months. Homelessness seems to contribute to demoralization, since the duration of this depressive state (11 weeks) corresponds to the length of homelessness (13 weeks). Furthermore, the respondents indicated that joblessness or lack of money were the main reasons for such feelings of demoralization.

The level of depressive symptomatology was also estimated for a subsample with the CES-D scale. This scale was specifically designed for measuring current depression symptomatology in community surveys. Using the usual cutting point of 16, 50 percent of this group would be classified as depressed; however, many studies (Myers & Weissman, 1980; Roberts & Vernon, 1983) have shown that the CES-D is a far from perfect predictor of diagnosable affective disorders. The high mean CES-D scores observed (mean = 18) are similar to those reported for alcoholic populations (Aneshensel, 1985). Since Fischer and her collaborators found that only 2 percent of their homeless sample obtained a Diagnostic Interview Schedule/Diagnostic and Statistical Manual III (DIS/DSM-III) diagnosis of affective disorder, the Los Angeles results should be interpreted with caution. Besides, as suggested by a four-year prospective study of a representative sample of the Los Angeles general population (Aneshensel, 1985), individuals classified as CES-D cases at any particular time are not homogenous in terms of the course of depressive symptoms. Among the depressed, two subgroups were identified: the isolated-episode cases and the recurrent-chronic cases. It is conceivable that the homeless population surveyed here followed patterns similar to those observed in the general population.

The majority of the sample (64 percent) indicated that they drank alcoholic beverages. From the modified version of the DIS on alcohol problems used in this study, it was estimated that the lifetime prevalence of alcohol abuse in this population was 26.0 percent, whereas the prevalence of alcohol dependence reached 19.0 percent. Analogously, 15 percent of the sample reported hospitalization for alcohol and/or drug-related problems in the previous 12 months.

Fischer and collaborators (1986) reported a 70.6 percent lifetime prevalence rate of DIS/DSM-III substance abuse/dependence diagnosis. This rate is superior to the 45.0 percent rate of prevalence of alcohol abuse and dependence reported here. This difference could be accounted for by the inclusion of other substances beside alcohol in Fischer's report. Also, the version of the instrument used in the Los Angeles study is probably more sensitive (fewer false negatives) because it incorporated fewer symptoms to report by the respondents. However, the 45 percent rate of alcohol abuse and dependence among the Los Angeles homeless sample needs to be evaluated against the fact that, nationally, one-third of the population are moderate or heavy drinkers (U.S. Department of Health and Human Services 1983, p. 2). In addition, it is estimated that only 3 to 4 percent of alcoholics in the United States live in skid row circumstances.

The general impression projected by these epidemiological findings is that homeless persons are in poor health, especially the homeless women. Other evidence collected from this survey suggests that poor health is not independent of the homeless situation, since 45 percent of the sample indicated that their health had worsened since they had been without a place to live.

Because in a community survey like this one, it is difficult to obtain objective measures of health from physician examinations, the health status of homeless individuals was estimated using a self-rating index of general health status. Respondents were asked, "How would you rate your health overall (poor, fair, good, excellent)?" One-third (33.4 percent) of the homeless persons interviewed rated their health as fair or poor. This is a large proportion compared with that in the Los Angeles population (22.5 percent) (Marcus et al., 1980) and with national estimates (National Center for Health Statistics, 1983).

Such self-reported indices have been widely used in health surveys. Ware and collaborators (1978) reviewed more than 30 empirical studies published from 1959 and 1976 and concluded, "Despite dissimilarities in measurement methods and populations studied, the weight of published evidence is consistent with the hypothesis that general health ratings are a valid measure of health status." Furthermore, recent longitudinal studies indicate that perceived health is a predictor of mortality, independent of physical health status (Massey & Shapiro, 1982; Singer, Garfinkel, & Cohen, 1976; Kaplan & Camacho, 1983).

Ware mentioned that the validity of perceived health is rarely addressed explicitly in published research. To test the construct validity of this health index in this homeless population, a stringent test was applied. Instead of looking at a multiplicity of associations between the index and the constructs it is supposed to measure, a multivariate analysis was conducted. This procedure minimizes the chance of finding spurious associations and takes into account the interrelations between predictors. If the index is a valid measure of general health, it should be substantially related to other measures of physical and mental health, and to health and illness behavior considered simultaneously.

Among the 12 variables analyzed, a chronic condition is the strongest correlate with perceived ill-health. This is congruent with Goldstein's study (1984), which suggests that perceived health status reflects the individual's sense of long-standing chronic illness. The second-best predictor of perceived health is contact with a physician for any acute physical condition. This variable, reflecting the severity of the acute condition, also supports the construct validity of perceived health.

Psychological distress also seems to contribute to the perception of ill-health among the homeless. The duration of depressive feelings and alcoholism symptomatology significantly improve our understanding of variation in self-perception in health status. The fact that the CES-D score is a strong predictor of perceived health for a subgroup of our population reveals the contribution of the psychological status to perceived health.

The data suggest, however, that physical health is the most important component of self-reported health status. Since only 26 percent of the variance observed in perceived health was accounted for by the 12 health variables considered, perceived health appears to be a very complex phenomenon among homeless individuals. The data suggest, however, that perceived health is a valid measure of general health. Considering also the simplicity of this kind of survey, perceived health status can be a cost-effective measure for future studies of homeless populations.

To estimate the relative importance of individual and social variables to perceived health, demographic and situational variables were also analyzed. Older homeless women with long periods of unemployment, low education, and low monthly income who have spent few nights in a shelter or mission and who have been victimized in the last six months —these were most likely to perceive themselves in poor health. Thus the data suggest that poor health is not a random phenomenon among the homeless, and the hierarchy among demographic and situational variables underlines the major contribution of unemployment to poor health. The homeless persons interviewed indicated that their financial situations had precipitated their poor health and not the inverse. They also noted that their ill-health did not prevent them from working. The majority of them were, in fact, part of the labor force.

SUMMARY

Based on the findings of the present study, as well as the findings of studies conducted in other cities, it appears that the contemporary urban homeless are younger, more nonwhite, and more recently homeless than previous generations of the chronically homeless, who were traditionally older white males. The data also suggest that Los Angeles homeless are not newcomers to Los Angeles, that they are socially isolated, and that in large proportion they are part of the labor force. A large number of the men interviewed were veterans.

In regard to the general health status of the homeless, the data indicate that respiratory infections and hypertension are the most prevalent problems. Because these conditions are self-reported, they could mask more serious conditions, and the hypertension is probably underestimated. Regarding the mental health of the homeless, the data indicate that demoralization is prevalent; yet comparisons of the findings with those of others suggest that major mental illness does not constitute the most prevalent mental condition in the population studied. Alcohol and drug abuse are still important problems.

A large segment of the homeless population studied did not consult or have access to any medical care. This implies that more effort should be devoted to epidemiological research among the homeless directly in the community. This is the best way to determine the health status of this population in order to direct the sparse resources available to the individuals at greatest risk. A perceived health status index, such as the one used in this survey, and a symptoms checklist, such as the CES-D, could be used as screening instruments in a two-stage epidemiological study.

The multivariate analysis findings suggest that improvement of the economic conditions of this population, plus increased accessibility to shelter and health care, could contribute to the improvement of the physical and mental health status of this homeless population. Special attention should be given to shelter for women.

Based on evidence from the present study and from other research concerned with the mental health status of the homeless, we still have imprecise estimates of type and prevalence of psychopathology in homeless populations. Mental illness is certainly an important public health issue and can explain part of the problem of homelessness. However, attempts to medicalize a complex socioeconomic problem like homelessness by approaching it only with a psychiatric model are one-sided and risk confusing consequences and causes. One should be careful not to make a metaphor of homelessness.

Understanding who the homeless are and where they come from must be the first step in proposing strategies to help them. Without the recognition that the homeless population is composed of several subgroups with different economic, health, and psychiatric needs, current policies will fail to deal with this growing social problem effectively.

Chapter 2

LIVING ON THE EDGE

An Evaluation of
Single Room Occupancy Residents
in Los Angeles

The traditional "skid row" homeless of the 1950s, 1960s, and 1970s were by and large not individuals without a roof over their heads—the homeless of past decades were essentially a sheltered population. The "socially terminal," that is, the elderly, the physically and mentally disabled, and the drug or alcohol dependent, along with displaced blacks from the south and Hispanic immigrants, were housed in skid row single room occupancy (SRO) hotels, more commonly referred to as "flophouses," or in "mission" shelters. It is important to recognize that homelessness involves many more than just those who lack "shelter," those who are literally living in the streets. The traditional skid row homeless of the post–World War II period were on the street but were "sheltered" in SRO hotels or rescue missions. The literature, however, correctly viewed them as homeless in a sociological sense. The difference in the 1980s is that many in some subpopulations of the homeless do not even have elementary shelter.

Although SRO hotels are a key source of shelter for the homeless, they must not be regarded as providing anything more than basic shelter; that is, they are not "homes." A 1985 report by the U.S. General Accounting Office offered the following definition of the homeless: "those persons who lack resources and community ties necessary to provide for their own adequate shelter" (U.S. GAO 1985, 5). Most observers agree that an SRO does not provide the kind of "adequate shelter" or community ties that constitute a home.

This was acknowledged by a congressional report on the homeless problem, which included residents of SROs to be among the homeless, as follows:

> For the purpose of this report, homeless people will be defined as those individuals and families who lack sufficient resources to provide for their own shelter. Such persons are found in emergency shelters, transition houses, Single Room Occupancy (SRO) hotels, the streets, subways, bus terminals, living under bridges and in abandoned buildings (U.S. House, Committee on Government Operations, 1985, p. 2).

In addition, a comprehensive review of 114 studies of the contemporary homeless found that 40 percent of the studies included SRO residents (Milburn & Watts, 1985–1986, p. 47).

The residents of SROs may be at the top of the stratification system of the contemporary homeless population; while nonetheless "homeless," they have at least elementary shelter. However, the majority of SRO residents suffer under conditions identical or similar to those of other homeless subgroups. These conditions include economic and social displacement; social and psychological isolation; and economic, political, social, and psychological disaffiliation.

Members of SRO populations constantly move back and forth between other subpopulations among the contemporary homeless. For example, homeless individuals without shelter in Los Angeles may qualify for a Department of Public Social Services emergency lodging voucher. Such a voucher entitles an individual to an SRO room in one of about 70 SRO hotels that have contracts with Los Angeles County. In January 1984, for example, an average of 1,211 persons were given SRO vouchers *each night* (Robertson, Ropers, & Boyer, 1984). Often

SRO rents must be paid weekly by the residents, so the many who run out of money before the end of the month are forced to live in mission shelters or on the streets until their welfare checks arrive.

Clearly, the concept of "homelessness" is sociologically broader than the concept of "shelterless." SRO residents are sociologically a subpopulation of the larger contemporary homeless population, and they can best be described as the "sheltered homeless."

SRO residents, like their unsheltered homeless counter-parts, have been removed from participation in mainstream economic institutions, often against their will, through the displacement caused by recession-level unemployment and underemployment. Others are forced to live in poverty because of low social security payments or welfare inadequate to keep them above the poverty line. The shrinking low-income housing market also prevents many from residing in communities other than skid rows.

A congressional committee has described the national scope of the SRO world in the late 1970s as follows:

> The number of hotels, the makeup of tenants, and the involvement of local governments and service agencies vary from city to city. But it is becoming abundantly clear that the SROs are not limited to large cities.
>
> SRO hotels have been found in communities as varied as: Charleston and Huntington, W.Va.; Big Stone Gap, Va.; Louisville and Lebanon, Ky.; Utica, Syracuse, and New York City, N.Y.; Des Moines, Cedar Falls, and Sioux City, Iowa; Portland, Oreg.; St. Louis, Mo.; San Diego, Santa Barbara, San Francisco, and Los Angeles, Calif.; Denver, Colo.; Seattle, Wash.; Detroit, Mich.; Minneapolis, Minn.; Chicago, Ill.; and Richmond, Va.
>
> Nationwide estimates of SRO populations are unavailable, but they have been made for several cities:
>
> - In Benton, Ill. (population 6,800), there is one SRO hotel with 30 units, 12 of which are occupied by elderly persons. In addition, there are three SRO rooming

houses with a total of 18 units, four of which are occupied by elderly persons.

- In Syracuse, N.Y. (population 197,000), there are seven SRO hotels (519 units)—four with absolutely no services and three with a combination of maid and linen services, television, and/or air conditioning. Nearly one-fourth of the rooms are occupied by elderly persons.

- In Denver, Colo. (population 500,000), a service agency has identified 42 residential hotels in the downtown area, ranging from 18 units to 194 units. Forty-eight percent of the occupants are over 60.

- In San Diego, Calif. (population 697,000), the core downtown area houses 32 residential hotels with upwards of 2,300 rooms. Approximately 59 percent of the rooms are rented on a permanent basis—over 6 months. The modal age of this census tract according to the 1970 census was 65–74 years for men and 75 years and over for females.

- In Portland, Oreg. (population 383,000), a sampling of four SROs reveals that 50 percent of the permanent occupants are over age 60.

- In New York City, N.Y. (population 7.8 million), 280 SRO's (approximately 50,000 rooms) have been identified by housing and service agencies. Unofficial estimates, however, indicate that as many as 8,000 SRO's may be located in New York City. A sampling of the buildings indicates that 18.3 percent of the population is over age 60.

SRO hotels are not exclusively for the elderly; in fact, the elderly do not normally constitute a majority of their clientele. However, research has indicated that the elderly are present in high proportions in the neighborhoods where SROs are generally found. Whereas, persons over age 65 constitute 10 percent of the total U.S. population, random surveys across the country have indicated that the single elderly population in center cities may range as high as 49 percent (U.S. Senate, Special Committee on Aging, 1978, pp. 2–3).

This chapter focuses on the SRO world of downtown Los Angeles. Data from a survey of 174 randomly selected SRO residents, legal declarations of SRO residents and of expert witnesses, and journalistic accounts document the displacement of the traditional SRO population and its replacement by subgroups of the new urban homeless.

SKID ROW

The Los Angeles County Department of Mental Health and the Department of Public Social Services have defined the boundaries of Los Angeles skid row as "an area bounded by First Street on the north, the Los Angeles River on the east, 16th Street on the south, and Broadway on the west" (1984, p. 6).

The sample of SRO residents examined in this chapter was drawn from the area referred to as Central City East, situated within the larger skid row boundaries indicated above. The boundaries of the Central City East area are First Street on the north, Central Avenue on the east, Main Street on the west, and Seventh Street on the south.

It has been estimated that there are approximately 15,000 SRO residents in the downtown Los Angeles area. Ten thousand of these SRO residents are located in skid row (Silvern & Schmunk, 1981, p. 1; de Wolfe, 1982).

Previous studies report that the traditional elderly white male SRO population is giving way to an influx of young Black males, Hispanic families, and single Hispanic males (Silvern & Schmunk, 1981, p. 2). For 1981, Silvern and Schmunk reported that average SRO rents in Los Angeles had increased over 30 percent in the twelve months since they had started their research. They found (for 1981) that "a typical hotel room in the Skid Row area currently rents for $190 to a Latino family, $140 to a single man, and $110 to an elderly person" (p. 2).

In the last several years, economic revitalization, conversion of SRO hotels to other purposes, and fires have contributed to displacement of some SRO residents. Between 1968 and 1981, approximately 29 hotels, containing 2,195 units, have been lost in the Los Angeles skid row area (Silvern & Schmunk, 1981, p. 4).

SRO hotels are the only housing many individuals can afford. Often they are the only housing choice available to elderly retired persons living on social security, pensions, or other forms of fixed income; young minority group persons; victims of high unemployment rates, or housing discrimination; and political and economic refugees from Central and Latin America.

The Los Angeles SROs were once essentially the domain of single, widowed, or divorced elderly persons, but in the 1980s it is not unusual to find whole families with small children living in them. It is estimated that 800 children, largely immigrants from Mexico and Central America, live with their families in SROs in skid row (Townsend, 1983).

Of course, SROs were not intended for family living; overcrowding of hotel rooms designated for single occupancy is a constant problem. Bill Wakeland, a Los Angeles Fire Department inspector, has stated, "The overcrowding issue is a bombshell, you can't ignore it. But it's a double-edged sword" ("City Confronts 'Bombshell'," 1983). If tenants are evicted for overcrowding, they have no choice but to move to another SRO hotel.

However, as repeatedly reported in the media, some landlords of SRO hotels neglect to make the improvements or repairs required by law to meet health, safety, and fire regulations (Hastings, 1983a, 1983b; Becklund, 1984; Burns, 1984; Furillo, 1984).

In the early 1980s the Los Angeles City Skid Row Task Force, under the leadership of City Attorney Ira Reiner, attempted to promote landlord compliance with health, safety, and fire regulations (Hastings 1983b); 75 criminal "slumlord" cases were filed in Municipal Court during the first ten months of 1984, and an additional 40 to 50 cases were under review. Many involve multiple violations of the Los Angeles Fire, Building and Safety, or Health Codes (Furillo, 1984).

The danger of hotel fires is perhaps the most persistent facing SRO residents—in 1982 a fire at the Dorothy Mae Hotel in Los Angeles killed 25 people. In addition to the deaths and injuries, hotel fires often leave SRO residents temporarily without shelter. In June 1982 a fire at the Lincoln Hotel in skid row forced the evacuation of all 150 residents for three days (Hastings, 1983b).

Fire danger is often present in SROs because of bad wiring, piles of rubbish, and the use of hot plates. If gas stoves are used for heating, they often create toxic fumes.

Crime and violence also plague the central city SRO hotels and neighborhoods. Los Angeles Police Officer Lamount explains, "We recover a lot of guns down here." From June to May 1983, robberies increased almost 50 percent. Lamount said, "Most of them are street robberies, mostly drunk roll types" ("Life in the Hotels," 1983).

Sometimes SRO residents organize to protect themselves from criminals and arsonists. Residents threatened with eviction at the Frostonya SRO Hotel organized a rent strike; women residents set up a housekeeping schedule to keep the hotel clean; and the men took turns being night watchmen.

Many long-term SRO residents are just one step away from being homeless on the streets. In September 1984 a judge ordered an SRO hotel closed and brought into conformity with health and fire codes within 60 days or destroyed. The tenants of this building, who were paying $325 a month for a tiny room without a kitchen or bathroom, contended that they would be on the streets if the hotel closed. One tenant was quoted as saying, "I don't have one penny on me—not one cent. If they put us out, we're going to be sittin' out there at the bus stop on the bench" (Burns, 1984).

Many homeless individuals who alternate between SROs and shelters for the homeless prefer the shelters. A 1984 fire at the Sunshine Mission for Women forced the relocation of the residents, by the Red Cross, into skid row hotels. As *Los Angeles Times* reporter Marita Hernandez reported, the displaced women "complain about the cockroaches and mice in their new quarters, muggings and theft." One former shelter resident suffered a nervous breakdown; another elderly woman, unable to feed and care for herself in the SRO, died (Hernandez, 1984).

Ironically, Los Angeles County, in an attempt to meet its

legal obligation to shelter homeless individuals, has a hotel system that issues vouchers, which are exchanged for rooms in SRO hotels. In October 1984 a lawsuit was filed against the County by the Legal Aid Foundation of Los Angeles, seeking

> an immediate order halting taxpayer funding by the defendant Board of Supervisors of four slum hotels to which the county consigns the homeless poor who have sought shelter from the county. Not far from the Courthouse and the County Hall of Administration there is an offensive reality which most citizens have never seen. Submitted with these moving papers are photographs of that reality, taken in recent weeks. Exhibit B. Also submitted are pictures of another kind—the descriptions of life in these hotels by dozens of men and women who have been compelled to live in them. These pictures are, like the reality of life in these hotels, a repulsive and unpleasant thing. These hotels—the Ellis, the Norbo, the Leonide and the Harold—are infested with rats and other disease-carrying vermin. They lack the bare essentials of heat, hot water, workable toilets, windows that close and doors that lock. They are strewn with trash, garbage, and worse. Some of them are literal firetraps. Plaintiffs also submit the declarations of three experts who went into each hotel in recent weeks: Brian E. Henderson, M.D., Chairman of the Department of Preventive Medicine at U.S.C. Medical School; Richard E. Hunter, A.I.A., an architect who sits on the Building Code Committee of the A.I.A.; and retired Fire Inspector William C. Wakeland of the Los Angeles City Fire Department. Their observations confirm those of the camera and the residents of the hotels: these buildings are not only ugly and unpleasant—they are also illegal.
>
> Perhaps more offensive is the fact that it is County taxpayers who subsidize these hotels, through the County's voucher hotel program. From January 1, 1983, County taxpayers have subsidized these four hotels in the amount of $350,899.20. These costs can be expected only to increase: in the past two months, the County has *increased* the rate paid to the owners of *each* of these hotels by forty-

five percent (45%). At least two of the hotels now deal exclusively with the County. For all practical purposes, these squalid slums are *County* facilities, operated in flagrant violation of the law, including the County's own Public Health Code. Yet, plaintiffs do not here seek an order which would compel the County to enforce its own laws. Plaintiffs seek only to end further subsidy of the violation of those laws with taxpayers' funds. (Paris, 1984).

The sworn testimony of two homeless persons (one an unemployed railroad worker who had become homeless; the other a 42-year-old woman) who had been sent by the county to its subsidized SRO hotels graphically illuminates the SRO world of Los Angeles. According to the unemployed railroad worker,

I was given two linens at the manager's office and brought to my room on the 3rd floor. The linens were dirty and dusty. I asked for towels and soap and was told I could get them next Thursday, a week later, the last day of my voucher.

The bed was filthy and black with body dirt. It smelled like urine. The smell came right from the sheets. I feel filthy now from having to sleep on it.

There is a bathtub in the hallway. You hope no one is sleeping in it so you can use it. There is dirt and scum crusted on it. You have to stuff newspapers in the drain to fill it with water. I washed out the sink, it was filthy. There were roaches in it and (it was) covered with dust and dirt.

There is no heat in the room and I was not issued a blanket. At night in bed if I turn on the light the bed will be filled with roaches. . . .

I shower at the mission. I just can't keep clean. Without being clean I can't look for work. Who wants to sit in front of a potential employer when you smell. And you just don't feel good. I can't expect an employer to take me seriously when I look like this. . . .

How do you expect me to function as a decent human being in indecent conditions (Paris, 1984)?

The 42-year-old woman stated,

> When I saw the room I cried and I was scared when I
> thought about sleeping there. There was poo poo in the
> toilet. The water was cut off so I couldn't flush the toilet.
> The sink had only cold water. The manager told me not to
> use the sink because it had a bad leak in the pipes. There
> was no hot water.
>
> There was pee stains and strong smells of pee in the
> mattress. I woke up in the middle of the night with bugs
> biting me. There were rats and mice running around. You
> could hear them gnawing and chewing in the walls.
>
> There was garbage on the floor. There were used and
> dirty rubbers around the bed.
>
> I tried my best to clean the room. I complained to the
> manager. I would have left then, but I had no place to go.
>
> I would rather sleep in this park than sleep in that
> nasty hotel. At least the bathroom and water fountain
> works in the park (Paris, 1984).

In a 1986 *Los Angeles Times* story, "Houses of Horror,"
reporter John Hurst described the "Slum Busters," members of
the Los Angeles Interagency Slum Housing Task Force who
have been trying to crack down on the owners of the worst
SRO slums. There were about 100 SRO buildings on the task
force case load in 1986; these buildings are described as the
"slums de la slums," of Los Angeles (Hurst, 1986).

In an article entitled "SROpportunism: Andy Raubeson's
Skid Row Clean-up Organization is a Slumlord," reporter Greg
Goldin of the *Los Angeles Weekly* alleged that the attempt by the
City of Los Angeles to give its skid row a facelift and preserve
its low-income SRO housing stock in 1986 is a "mirage" (Gol-
din, 1986). Similar questions were raised by the *Los Angeles
Times* in a subsequent article (Abrams, 1986).

The city's SRO Housing Corporation, using Community
Redevelopment Agency monies, purchased "nine ramshackle,
insect-infested, tinder box hotels" in skid row. Reporter Goldin
later wrote,

Eight of the nine hotels are either off the market or remain the same dismal dumps of human indignity they were $11 million ago. SRO's principal beneficiary so far seems to be Andy Raubeson, who gets a $90,000 annual salary, a city-underwritten frequent-flyer program, and an SRO van to toodle around Skid Row. Compare that to the $228 per month SRO tenants must scrape by on.

Six of the nine hotels are closed for "renovation." Only one, the Florence, has been refurbished and re-opened, and then only after 18 months of delays (Goldin, 1986).

The homeless themselves are critical of Mayor Tom Bradley's policy of cleaning up skid row and sheltering the homeless in city-run SROs. The Los Angeles Union of the Homeless, one of several self-help organizations of the homeless that have attempted to build street communities run for and by the homeless, pointed out in its magazine *LOVE: Learning, Organizing, Voting and Employment* that

the failure of the Bradley administration can be gauged in the short-sightedness of the very name of this strategic corporation, *single-room occupancy*. Where is it written that single-room occupancy is the solution to homelessness?. . .

How in the world does the silly phrase "single-room occupancy" in any way relate to this problem? It doesn't, and Andy Raubeson should resign from running this corporation because he refuses to acknowledge that, as structured, SRO is a guaranteed failure ("Failure of the City," 1987, p. 2).

A *Los Angeles Times* article, in June of 1987, also reported on the growing controversy surrounding the SRO Housing Corporation.

For about the past year, SRO has been a source of ire for some other social service providers on Skid Row. Over the past few months their criticisms have intensified—mainly that the agency has moved too slowly in renovation and has exacerbated the housing shortage by closing hotels to fix them up. The agency's executive director, Andy Raubeson, also has become more of a target, primarily because he supported city action against homeless encampments earlier this year (Abrams, 1987b).

EVALUATION

Methodology

Thirty SRO hotels were randomly selected from a list of all SRO hotels in the Los Angeles Central City area, excluding family hotels. Room numbering systems were obtained for each hotel, and a random selection of rooms was then produced for inclusion in the survey. A total of 280 rooms were selected through this procedure, and 174 residents were interviewed. The resulting gross response rate is 62 percent. The interviewers were paid and trained by the SRO Housing Corporation of Los Angeles.

A questionnaire was developed containing 145 items covering several dimensions of SRO life. These dimensions include:

demographics,
residential choice and patterns,
leisure/recreational activities,
business/shopping activities,
health status and health care utilization,
life satisfaction,
social support,
employment/unemployment status and history,
economic status,
alcohol use and alcohol treatment utilization, and
social services utilization.

This questionnaire was largely derived from the research instrument utilized in the 1980 Burnside Portland SRO Study

(Ille, 1980). Drafts of the proposed instrument were circulated to knowledgeable individuals for comment before finalization of the instrument.

Ten interviewers were hired; their training consisted of a five-hour training session. The interviewers were each given an interviewer study and instructional packet and equipped with interview forms, pencils, clipboard, map of Central City East, letter of introduction, and letters to leave in mailboxes.

Paired interviewers approached the randomly preselected SRO rooms. If a resident refused to be interviewed, the interviewers noted the reason and moved on to the next selected room number. Residents unable to respond because of intoxication or other physical conditions were informed that an interviewer would return at a later date. If no response was given at a knock on the room door, the interviewers checked with the manager or clerk to determine whether the room was vacant; if it was, an alternate room number was chosen. If the rooms were occupied but their tenants were not present at the time of initial contact, a letter was left informing them that an interviewer would return later. For Spanish-speaking-only residents, a Spanish version of the interview was conducted if the interviewer was bilingual, or the resident was informed that a Spanish-speaking interviewer would return later.

All of the interviews were conducted between 20 August, 1984 and 7 September, 1984. Respondents who completed an interview were paid $5.00.

Results

Previous generations of skid row and SRO homeless had been found to be dominated by elderly, unattached, retired, often disabled white males (Bogue, 1963; Wallace, 1965; Bahr, 1973). Nationally, skid row populations of the 1980s, however, are increasingly younger and less white (Ropers & Robertson, 1984a and 1984b; Miller 1982).

The changing character of skid row populations is evident in the Los Angeles SRO sample. In 1981 Silvern and Schmunk reported that over 25 percent of the Los Angeles skid row SRO residents were elderly males, and in a 1973 study of the Los

Angeles skid row population, O'Kane (1973) found 38% of her sample were over 50 years of age. But evidence is growing, both from the data of the Los Angeles sample and other studies, that, as are similar groups across the country, the Los Angeles skid row SRO elderly population is declining and a younger, nonwhite population is increasing.

Only 14.9 percent of the Los Angeles SRO residents sampled are 60 years or older, while nearly half (45.4 percent) are under the age of forty. (See Table 2.1.) The mean age of the present sample is 43, and the range is from 18 to 88. Nationally, individuals aged 65 or older constitute 10 percent of the population; only 9 percent of the present SRO sample are 65 or older. Miller's 1982 survey of skid rows documented the "skid row explosion," characterized by the increasing influx of younger men into skid row areas across the country. Increases in the younger male skid row population have been found to be historically linked to economic depressions and recessions (Miller, 1982, pp. 21–22).

The vast majority of the Los Angeles SRO sample is male (91.4 percent).This finding is consistent with other studies on SRO residents.

The racial composition of the sample is perhaps indicative of the changing composition of the Los Angeles skid row population, which, like other skid row populations, in past decades was populated largely by older white males. The 1980s are witnessing the growth of an increasingly nonwhite skid row population in Los Angeles and across the country (Ropers, 1985a).

Of the present sample, 63 percent are nonwhite, 46.8 percent Black, 13.3 percent Hispanic, 1.7 percent Asian, and 1.2 percent Native American. (See Table 2.1.) While Blacks make up only 12 percent of the Los Angeles County population, they are disproportionately represented among the unemployed and the homeless. (See Table 2.2.) Blacks were the youngest group in our SRO sample; the mean age for Blacks was 37, compared with 51 for whites, 42 for Hispanics, and 54 for others. Race and age are apparently associated variables ($r = .39$), with Blacks and Hispanics significantly younger than whites and others.

TABLE 2.1
Select Characteristics of SRO Sample
(in percentage)

Age		Residency in Skid Row	
28 or less	17.8	1 year or less	37.0
29 to 39	27.6	13 months to 5 years	36.0
40 to 59	39.7	More than 5 years	27.0
60+	14.9		
	(n = 174)		(n = 174)
Sex		**Years lived in present hotel**	
Male	91.4	1 year or less	62.0
Female	8.6	13 months to 2 years	13.0
	(n = 174)	25 months or more	25.0
			(n = 174)
Race			
White	37.0	**Health rating**	
Black	46.8	Good	52.0
Hispanic	13.3	Fair	32.0
Asian	1.7	Poor	16.0
Native American	1.2		(n = 174)
	(n = 173)		
		Psychiatric Hospitalization	
Marital status		Yes	9.8
Married	6.4	No	90.2
Widowed	6.4		(n = 174)
Separated	9.2		
Divorced	23.7	**Drinking Behavior**	
Live with someone	1.2	Abstainer	46.0
Never married	53.2	Light drinker	5.0
	(n = 173)	Moderate drinker	17.0
		Heavy drinker	30.0
Education			(n = 171)
Less than high school	39.9		
High school diploma	39.3	**Veteran**	
Some college or more	20.8	Yes	40.0
	(n = 173)	No	60.0
			(n = 173)

TABLE 2.2

Race, Poverty, Unemployment, Homelessness and SRO Residents in Los Angeles

	Los Angeles County Population		Persons below Poverty Line		Unemployment 1983	Homeless Sample		SRO Residents Sample	
	n	%	n	%	%	n	%	n	%
White	3,867,404	53.0	285,564	7.4	9.0	133	49	64	37.0
Black	923,970	12.6	212,992	23.4	16.4	87	32	81	46.8
Hispanic	2,043,004	26.0	419,150	20.5	12.4	28	10	23	13.3
Asian	450,868	6.0	57,724	12.8	—	2	1	3	1.7
Native American	53,581	1.4	9,101	17.0	—	13	6	2	1.2
Other	—	—	—	—	—	6	2	—	—
TOTAL	7,338,827		984,531			269		174	

SOURCES: Los Angeles County population, from *Summary characteristics for governmental units and standard metropolitan statistical areas,* California PHC 80–361 (Washington, DC: U.S. Department of Commerce, Bureau of the Census, 1982); 1983 unemployment, from *Annual planning information, Los Angeles–Long Beach, SMSA 1984–85* (Sacramento, CA: State of California, Department of Employment Development, 1984); homeless sample, from R. H. Ropers, The Rise of the New Urban Homeless, *Public Affairs Report* (Berkeley: University of California, Institute of Governmental Studies) 26(1985, 5&6).

The majority of the Los Angeles SRO sample (53 percent) had never been married; however, most of the never-married group (63 percent) were under the age of 39. However, 7.6 percent of the sample were married or living with someone, and the remaining 39.4 percent had been married, but were now widowed (6.4 percent), divorced (23.7 percent), or separated (9.2 percent).

Many among the SRO sample (60 percent) had a high school education or better, and this compares well with the Los Angeles County percentage of 70 percent. Blacks had the highest percentage (70 percent) of those who had completed high school or more, compared with whites (59.4 percent), Hispanics (30.3 percent), and others (60 percent).

Of the sample, 40 percent were veterans; all of the veterans are males. A large minority (37 percent) of the sample were relatively new residents of Los Angeles' skid row, and a majority (62 percent) had lived in their present SRO hotel a year or less. Nearly half (48 percent) indicated poor or fair health status, and a very small minority (9.8 percent) reported having been hospitalized for psychiatric reasons.

A large group (46 percent) were abstainers from alcohol, while only 30 percent described themselves as heavy drinkers.

Some interesting patterns emerge when the mean number of years lived in Los Angeles, in skid row, and in present SRO hotel are compared across racial groups. Blacks and Hispanics were significantly more recent arrivals than whites—to Los Angeles, to skid row, and to their present hotels. (See Table 2.3.)

TABLE 2.3
Select Residential Means, by Race

	White	Black	Hispanic	Other	F	p
Years lived in Los Angeles metropolitan area	15.0	9.52	9.29	19.8	3.16	≤.05
Years lived in Central City East (Skid Row)	8.31	3.45	5.79	6.40	4.03	≤.01
Years lived in present hotel	3.69	1.37	2.06	3.76	3.38	≤.01
Amount of rent	$194	$202	$180	$126	2.36	≤.07

Economic Status

Skid row populations have always varied with the state of the economy. As the ranks of the unemployed grow, so does the number of residents of skid row. Some researchers hold that skid rows have always been dumping grounds for unemployed, unattached males and for discarded elderly, retired, or disabled workers.

The findings from the sample support those interpretations. Only 21.3 percent were presently working at a paid job, and 78.7 percent were without employment. However, this 78.7 percent is not the same as the unemployment rate among the sample. The unemployment rate is derived as the percentage unemployed in the labor force (those working and those seeking work) (Ille, 1980).

Of those not working, 11.3 percent($n = 15$) were retired; 20.3 percent ($n = 27$) were disabled; and 3 percent ($n = 4$) did not want work. Others (42.9 percent, $n = 57$) were looking for work; 6 percent ($n = 8$) could not find a job; 7.5 percent ($n = 10$) had a temporary illness, and 9 percent ($n = 12$) reported "other" as a reason for not working.

If we exclude the 58 individuals who are not working because they were retired, disabled, did not want work, or reported "other" reasons from the total sample n, we are left with 116 individuals of the sample in the work force, 37 of whom were presently working. The resulting unemployment for this SRO sample is 68 percent, which is at least three times higher than the Los Angeles County unemployment rate.

By the same formula, the rate for able-bodied whites in the present sample was 59 percent, Blacks 69 percent, and Hispanics 33 percent. These rates are sharply higher than the rates for these respective groups countywide.

Of those working, 20 percent were underemployed, working only part time. Another 20 percent have only temporary full-time jobs, and 28.6 percent responded to the "other" category. Only 31.4 percent ($n = 11$) of those working reported having a full-time steady job (only 6 percent of the total sample). When those who were able to work were asked what kind of work they would prefer, 88.6 percent said they would prefer full-time, steady work. Many of these (88.9 percent) were interested in job training, 41.3 percent in professional/technical training, 20 percent in clerical training, and 17.5 percent in craftsmanship training.

Job Type

Among those with jobs ($n = 36$), 63.9 percent were working as laborers; 25 percent as service workers; 5.1 percent as operatives, 2.8 percent as clerical workers; and 2.8 percent in professional/technical jobs. However, among the entire sample who answered the question, "What did you do in your last job?" ($n = 128$), a greater diversity of occupations is presented. Reporting on their last job, the respondents indicated that 26.6 percent had been service workers, 22.7 percent were laborers, 15.6 percent operatives, 14.8 percent professional/technical, 10.2 percent craftsmen, 7.8 percent clerical workers, and 1.6 percent farm laborers.

Income

The mean monthly income of the sample ($n = 167$) was $331 and the median $256. The range of monthly incomes was 0 to $2,000; however, 17 individuals indicated that they received no income at all, and only one reported an income of $2,000.

Not surprisingly, given the high unemployment rate among the sample, only 26.7% received income from wages. Aside from wages, the leading source of income was public assistance (52 percent), followed by social security (16 percent), supplemental social security insurance (S.S.I., 15.3 percent), veterans' pensions (7.3 percent), and other pensions (2.7%). Despite the high rate of unemployment, only 0.7 percent ($n = 1$) of the sample was receiving unemployment insurance.

When asked if they were out of money at the end of the month, 51.7 percent reported "all the time," 28.7 percent "some of the time," 9.2% "not usually," and 10.3 percent "never." Asked if they had had to borrow money in the previous month, 47.1 percent responded affirmatively. Over half of the residents supplemented their income by receiving food stamps.

Race

Mean monthly income was significantly related to race. Blacks had the lowest mean income ($265), and "others" (60 percent were Asian) had the highest mean income ($428). Whites and others received more income from Social Security, S.S.I., and veterans' pensions than other groups. (See Table 2.4.) Blacks received more public assistance (62.5 percent) than whites (36.5 percent), Hispanics (30.4 percent), or others (40 percent).

While there are no significant differences between race and reasons for not working, more Blacks (51.5 percent) and Hispanics (58.8 percent) were looking for work than whites (27.1 percent) or others (25 percent).

DISCUSSION

It was not unexpected that the economic status of SRO residents was precarious; in many cases it is the economic instability of these individuals that brings them to skid row SRO living in the first place. The data clearly support the view that the Los Angeles skid row SRO residents were predominantly displaced, disabled, or retired workers. The majority of the displaced were unemployed young Blacks who were looking for work and receiving public assistance in the interim. Others were older, mostly white, disabled or retired workers living on Social Security, S.S.I., and pensions. Compared with other groups, the Hispanics among this SRO sample were more likely to be working and not receiving any public assistance.

Overall, most of those able to work were looking for work and receptive to job training programs. But given the highest unemployment rates since the end of World War II, it is not surprising to have found so many among the sample unemployed.

TABLE 2.4
Economic Status by Race
(in percentage)

	White	Black	Hispanic	Other	F	p
Mean Income	395	265	350	428	3.94	≤.01
Sources of Income						
Wages						NS
Yes	23.8%	21.3%	34.8%	20.0%		
No	76.2	78.8	65.2	80.0		
	(n = 63)	(n = 80)	(n = 23)	(n = 5)		
Social Security					13.57	≤.01
Yes	25.4%	6.3%	8.7%	40.0%		
No	74.6	93.8	91.3	60.0		
	(n = 63)	(n = 80)	(n = 23)	(n = 5)		
S.S.I.					10.00	≤.01
Yes	23.8%	6.3%	8.7%	20.0%		
No	76.2	93.8	91.3	80.0		
	(n = 63)	(n = 80)	(n = 23)	(n = 5)		
Veterans pension					7.58	≤.05
Yes	11.1%	1.3%	8.7%	20.0%		
No	88.9	98.8	91.3	80.0		
	(n = 63)	(n = 80)	(n = 23)	(n = 5)		
Pension						NS
Yes	3.2%	1.3%	4.3%	0%		
No	96.8	98.8	95.7	100.0		
	(n = 63)	(n = 80)	(n = 23)	(n = 5)		

Public Assistance					13.04	≤.01
Yes	36.5%	62.5%	30.4%	40.0%		
No	63.5	37.5	69.6	60.0		
	(n = 63)	(n = 80)	(n = 23)	(n = 5)		
Unemployment Insurance						NS
Yes	1.6%	0%	4.3%	0%		
No	98.4	100.0	95.7	100.0		
	(n = 63)	(n = 80)	(n = 23)	(n = 5)		
Present job type						NS
Steady full-time	21.4%	27.8%	66.7%	0%		
Temporary full-time	28.6	11.1	33.3	100.0		
Part-time	28.6	16.7	0	0		
Other	21.4	44.4	0	0		
	(n = 14)	(n = 10)	(n = 6)	(n = 1)		
Reason not working						NS
Retired	16.7%	6.1%	11.8%	25.0%		
Disability	31.3	15.2	11.8	25.0		
Temporary illness	6.3	7.6	5.9	25.0		
Looking for job	27.1	51.5	58.8	25.0		
Do not want work	6.3	1.5	0	0		
Can't find job	4.2	7.6	5.9	0		
Other	8.3	10.6	5.9	0		
	(n = 48)	(n = 66)	(n = 17)	(n = 4)		

Chapter 3

THE RISE OF THE
NEW URBAN HOMELESS

Social disorganization is a condition all societies experience at one time or another. Wars, civil wars, revolutions, economic depressions, and technological changes are examples of the types of events that disrupt the dominant normative and structural framework of a society. Most social systems, unless completely destroyed in the process of social disruption, manage to restore some degree of equilibrium after major upheavals. Often restoration of the social order requires a major realignment of social forces and power, a changing of political and economic priorities, and modified styles of living for its members. From the individual's perspective, social disruption may often result in personal disorganization. The breakdown of social roles and expectations may leave the individual in both an objective and a subjective state of disorientation. Even when the individual gets a "handle" on the disorienting condition, what follows is often a psychologically and physically stressful period of adjustment to newly emerging social roles and expectations.

Of all the possible events that could happen to an individual as a result of social disruption, short of death, homelessness is perhaps the most devastating form of personal and social disorganization. To have a home is to be anchored to some form of social network and to have a basis for establishing other social supports.

In its 200-year history, American society has known several periods of major social disorganization. However, massive homelessness was first documented as a result of the Civil War (Bruns, 1980, p. 7).

THE CIVIL WAR AND THE INDUSTRIALIZATION OF AMERICA

The Civil War brought about extensive social dislocation and movement of populations. Thousands of civilians were displaced from their homes, and in many cases, traditional patterns of social interaction were destroyed. After the war, many Union and Confederate soldiers had to forage their way home on their own resources. Some of these veterans, finding no jobs available for them in the postwar economy, continued their homeless nomadic existence. The term "hobo" probably is derived from "*ho*meward *bo*und," the answer given by soldiers after the Civil War when asked where they were going (Bruns, 1980, p. 12).

The latter part of the nineteenth century was also a time of intensified industrialization in the East, where machinery increasingly began to displace workers in the mills, mines, and factories. Some of these displaced workers hoped to find jobs in the Midwest and West, where there were job opportunities in the growing railroad, timber, mining, and agricultural industries. These jobs required unattached and mobile workers who could adjust to the seasonal or transitory nature of the work.

While in the popular mind the terms hobo, bum, and tramp are synonymous, there are important distinctions among them. As R. Bruns points out, in the vernacular of the road a "hobo" is a migratory worker, a "tramp" is a migratory non-worker, and a "bum" is a nonmigratory nonworker. The hobos of the late nineteenth and early twentieth centuries became the "working class of the road" (1980, p. 11).

Post–Civil War industrial expansion was characterized by economic depressions, which also contributed to late-nineteenth-century homelessness (Vander Kooi, 1971, p. 306; Bahr, 1973, p. 35). Economic and political disruption in Europe and the promise of opportunity in America brought hundreds of thousands of immigrants to America's shores. Unable to find jobs in the settled industrial East, many of the immigrants also became workers of the road (Bruns, 1980, p. 7).

THE EMERGENCE OF SKID ROW

The best-known geographical concentrations of homeless persons, at least since the period after the Civil War, have been the urban areas known as "skid rows." Wallace believes that skid rows emerged as distinctive urban areas in the early 1870s (1965, p. 16). Today every major American city appears to have its own skid row, marked by particular economic, social, and housing characteristics. Donald J. Bogue, in his study of American skid rows, has given us what has become the classic description of a skid row area.

> The term "Skid Row" has come to denote a district in the city where there is a concentration of substandard hotels and rooming houses charging very low rates and catering primarily to men with low incomes. These hotels are intermingled with numerous taverns, employment agencies offering jobs as unskilled laborers, restaurants serving low-cost meals, pawnshops and secondhand stores, and missions that daily provide a free meal after the service. . . . Most are frequently located near the Business District and also near a factory district or major heavy transportation facilities such as a waterfront, freight yards, or a trucking and storage depot (1963, p. 1).

The expression "skid row" is derived from "Skid Road," which originally referred to Yessler Way in downtown Seattle. In the latter part of the nineteenth century, the Northwestern loggers would utilize various streets by freezing them over, by laying logs across them, or by actually greasing them to facilitate the movement of lumber down to waterways (Vander Kooi, 1971, p. 305; Miller, 1982, p. 2; Bahr, 1973, p. 3). The term "skid row" later came to connote not only the downward movement of timber, but also the apparent downward social mobility of skid row's inhabitants.

Some views of skid row claim that skid rows emerged and persisted because they were depositories of deviants, drunks, addicts, and social misfits. Contrary to this perspective is an urban ecological analysis, which examines the emergence and persistence of skid rows in terms of their social and economic functions for the larger society. Since their emergence, skid rows have been a repository of reserve labor and a depository for discarded elderly, disabled, and unemployed workers. In the last quarter of the nineteenth century and the early part of the twentieth century, skid rows were a marketplace for "unattached nonpermanent" workers. The lumber, railroad, and agricultural industries required a labor pool of mobile, single men. The bars, cheap lodginghouses, brothels, all-night theaters, pawnshops, and so on that characterized skid row came into existence and flourished to accommodate this labor pool. The skid row areas and the services they provided became known to these workers as the "main stem" (Vander Kooi, 1971, pp. 305–307).

The rise and history of skid row is inseparable from the ebb and flow of the larger economy and from social upheavals such as war. Skid row populations increased during the economic depressions of 1873, 1885, 1930–1938, and after each major war (Vander Kooi, 1971, p. 306; Bogue, 1963, p. 12; Bahr, 1973, p. 49). The economic panic of 1873, referred to as "Black September," produced unemployment rates of between 30 and 40 percent. Wallace points out that the depression of 1873, "turned [homelessness] into a way of life which was to give birth to that same familiar section in most major American cities called skid row" (1965, p. 15). In addition to being a habitat for a particular labor pool, skid row also became the place where society deposited its unwanted unemployed, physically and mentally disabled, and retired workers.

As the period of intense industrialization of the economy

after the Civil War and into the early part of the twentieth century came to an end and technological changes reduced the need for manual laborers, the stage was set for changes in the composition of the skid row population. The programs of the New Deal, the U.S. entry into World War II, and the postwar economic boom emptied skid rows of able-bodied unemployed men. For example, during World War II the Los Angeles skid row was emptied of all its able-bodied men. Union Rescue Mission historian Helga Henry wrote, "Defense plants swept the streets of all but decrepit men; only a small minority still roamed about, too engulfed by old age or chronic infirmity to do anything" (1955, p. 143). While skid row still provided a labor pool of temporary manual workers and agricultural workers, by the mid-1950s the skid row populations of the nation were dominated by retired, disabled, elderly white men on welfare. Henry described the homeless of the Los Angeles skid row in the 1950s, writing, "The young are there, prematurely old. But especially everywhere are the middle-aged and the elderly, like so many blighted blossoms once bursting in beauty and promise, now wilted, drooped, broken, diseased (1955, p. 180).

But why do society's unwanted workers become concentrated in skid row areas? After reviewing the conditions of skid rows in 45 cities, Bogue came up with a list of various reasons why people may come to live in skid row. Among the reasons listed were factors such as inexpensive lodging and food, employment opportunities for laborers, the welfare activities of missions, and the fact that they were sent there by social agencies to save money (1963, p. 75).

From the 1960s to the early 1980s, social scientists were describing and celebrating the decline of skid row populations and areas (Lee, 1980; Miller, 1982; Bogue, 1963; Bahr, 1973). Some suggested a "national-prosperity" view (Bahr, 1973, p. 49) that since skid rows are barometers of the economy and since the U.S. economy was in a "permanent" boom period during the 1960s, skid rows would naturally decline. Increasing welfare benefits and urban renewal programs were also thought to contribute to the decline of skid row.

Bogue estimated that in 1950 there had been 100,000

homeless across the country (1963, p. 8). In 1984 HUD estimated a maximum of 350,000 homeless, while the National
Coalition for the Homeless put the number between 2,000,000
and 3,000,000. Reports from major cities across the nation
indicate that homeless populations are growing. Skid row areas
have not only survived but are overflowing. Homeless people
can be seen in all parts of our cities, not only on skid row,
but also in the middle-class and even upper-class residential
neighborhoods.

THE TRICKLE-DOWN MISERY OF THE 1980s

The lack of low-income housing is often cited as the main
cause of contemporary homelessness, compounded by current
economic and political trends. The factors that cause individuals to become homeless are, however, always multiple and
interrelated. These include unemployment and eviction, ineli-
gibility for welfare, physical or mental disability, and divorce or
domestic violence. But the common denominator confronting
all potentially homeless people is the scarcity of low-income
housing.

The rise in the number of new urban homeless in the
1980s is also stimulated both directly and indirectly by economic and social processes in operation since the late 1960s.
Thus other contributing factors are changes in the occupational structure through "deindustrialization," recession-level
unemployment, increasing poverty and cutbacks in social welfare programs, increasing family instability, and the deinstitutionalization of mental patients. All of these processes have
been exacerbated by the political policies and strategies of the
Reagan administration. While the Reagan administration did
not bring about the long-term economic and social transformations occurring in the United States, it is responsible for the
enormous cutbacks in domestic social welfare programs, just at
the time increases are needed most.

Despite political rhetoric about limited recovery, in the
early 1980s the economy experienced the highest unemployment rates since the 1930s. Disinvestment in U.S. industries

resulted in numerous plant shutdowns and slowdowns, runaway shops (industries leaving the United States), and relatively high interest rates. Conservative political reforms compounded these economic problems, resulting in enormous cutbacks in social welfare programs, including government subsidy of low-income housing.

Consequently, the 1983 poverty rate reached an 18-year high. Family instability has been on the increase throughout this period, and more female-headed families live in poverty than ever before. Reduced funding for state hospitals has led to the deinstitutionalization of mental patients, some of whom end up without work and on the streets.

The high disproportionate representation of blacks among the homeless suggests that all of these factors, except perhaps deinstitutionalization, have affected blacks and other minorities more severely than whites. Each one of these factors will be discussed with a special focus on their impact on blacks, who are the minority group most overrepresented among the new urban homeless.

THE HOUSING CRISIS

According to a recent congressional review of the causes of homelessness, "the scarcity of low-income housing appears to be the main cause of homelessness. Poor people simply cannot afford . . . [the] majority of available housing in the United States" (U.S. House, Committee on Government Operations, 1985, p. 3).

In the 1980s, skyrocketing increases in rents and mortgage interest rates probably have contributed most directly to increasing homelessness, along with urban renewal programs that are disrupting skid row areas. Many of the SRO buildings are being destroyed or converted into condominiums. In New York City, for example, 87 percent of the SROs were lost to urban renewal between 1970 and 1980, and the rent-income ratio (the proportion of income that goes to rent), rose from an average of 19 percent in 1950 until, by 1985, nearly half of the residents paid 30 percent of their income for rent and three out of ten paid 40 percent. The rent-income ratio was highest for the poor (Berger, 1985).

New York City has had a housing shortage since World War II, but in the 1980s the vacancy rates have declined even further. In 1978 the vacancy rate (percent of housing units vacant compared to all units) was 2.95 percent, but it fell to only 2.04 percent in 1984. The number of homeless families housed in hotel rooms paid for by New York City was 1,400 in 1983, but the number had grown to 3,285 by late 1984. The New York City Housing Authority estimates that about 10 percent of all families in 1983 were "doubling up" (more than one family living in a single unit; Berger, 1985).

A report by the California Homeless Coalition attributes part of the homeless problem to lack of affordable housing, citing a 1978 California Department of Housing and Community Development estimate that "there were almost twice as many low-income renter households as there were rental units at an affordable price range" (Waters, 1984).

In addition, many persons are displaced through eviction. In 1983 the number of evictions in San Francisco was 5,800. The average number of evictions in central Los Angeles for 1983 and 1984 was close to 35,000.

Chester Hartman, a national authority on housing, believes the Reagan administration is reversing 50 years of federal government aid in providing housing for the poor. He cites the following policies as contributing to contemporary homelessness: ending existing new construction programs for lower-income households; sloughing off existing lower-income housing developments through deterioration, demolition, conversion, or sale; extracting ever-larger portions of lower-income household budgets as payment required for federally subsidized housing; and introducing a new housing allowance program as the primary federal housing tool (Hartman, 1982, p. 141).

Nationally, the median gross rent rose 101 percent between 1968 and 1979, while renters' median incomes rose only 59 percent. The proportion of income spent on rent also increased during the 1970s. In 1970, 40 percent of renters were paying 25 percent of their income for housing and 25 percent of renters were paying 35 percent or more; by the early 1980s, 53 percent of renters paid 25 percent of their income for housing, and 33 percent of renters paid 35 percent or more (Hartman, 1983, pp. 1–25).

A 1985 U.S. General Accounting Office report explained the decline of the low-income housing supply as a result of

> high interest rates, greater profits available for other types of construction, rent control, neighborhood opposition to public housing, declining federal subsidies for both developers and tenants, downtown redevelopment, condominium conversion, income tax provisions and high property taxes encouraging owner abandonment of housing, and neighborhood crime, including arson (GAO, 1985, p. 25).

A 1986 national survey of 25 major U.S. cities, conducted by the United States Conference of Mayors, found that demand for assisted housing by low-income households had increased in 88 percent of the cities surveyed. (See Table 3.1.) Eighteen months is the average waiting period for assisted housing, from the beginning of the application process until assistance is granted. In 68 percent of the cities surveyed, applications for housing assistance are no longer accepted because the waiting lists are too long, and only an average of 30 percent of qualified low-income families are served by assisted housing programs. Finally, in 54 percent of the cities, the stock of safe, decent, and affordable rental housing has decreased.

The disproportionate number of blacks among the homeless may also be the result of the documented housing discrimination facing minorities. Alphonso Pinkney, in his book *The Myth of Black Progress*, contends that "housing is one of the areas in which black people have faced greatest discrimination" (1984, 70). Pinkney quotes the Department of Housing and Urban Development's 1976 study of housing for blacks as stating,

> The housing of blacks is more than twice as often physically flawed as is the housing of the total population. And

to live in adequate accommodations, a black household must spend a larger portion of its income in housing than the average householder needs to (Pinkney, 1984, p. 70).

Pinkney also cites a 1978 HUD study on discrimination in housing that

> found that Blacks looking for apartments to rent encounter discrimination three out of four times. And Blacks in the market to purchase a house were discriminated against two out of three times" (1984, p. 70).

Pinkney concluded his analysis of discrimination in housing by stating,

> Discrimination in housing is a function of many factors, including broker practices and years of ingrained cultural attitudes. But one of the major causes is the lack of enforcement of the law by the Department of Housing and Urban Development. The department argues, on the other hand, that new laws are necessary to curb this, the most widely practiced form of discrimination (p. 71).

John Calmore, in his 1986 study of housing policies and black Americans, states,

> The 'disadvantageous distinction' of being black in America probably presents its most diverse, complex, and intractable problems in our attempts to secure viable property rights and housing opportunities (p. 115).

Current federal government housing policies, in addition to housing discrimination, have probably also contributed to the homelessness of many blacks. Calmore contends that

> the "center-piece" of the nation's housing program under Reagan has dwindled to an inadequate private market voucher system that reduces the low-income housing prob-

TABLE 3.1
City Data on Housing

City	Assisted Housing Demand 1986	Average Wait in Months	Stopped Accepting Applications	Low-Income Households Served (in percentage)	Affordable Housing Stock in Last Five Years
Boston	increased	60	yes	70	decreased
Charleston, S.C.	increased	9–12	yes	35	same
Chicago	increased	(a)	yes	45	increased
Cleveland	increased	12	yes	37	increased
Denver	increased	4	yes	—	increased
Detroit	increased	1–2	no	—	increased
Hartford	increased	3–12	yes	—	increased
Kansas City	increased	6	yes	12	decreased
Los Angeles	increased	18	yes	12	increased
Louisville	increased	36	yes	—	same
Minneapolis	increased	3	no	30	decreased
Nashville	increased	3–36	yes	70	decreased

New Orleans	increased	24(b)	no	—	same
New York City	increased	24	no	10	decreased
Norfolk	same	8–12	no	—	decreased
Philadelphia	increased	(c)	yes	—	decreased
Phoenix	same	24	yes	15	increased
Portland	increased	(d)	yes	30	same
Salt Lake City	increased	9	no	29	decreased
San Antonio	increased	(e)	yes	10	decreased
San Francisco	increased	30	yes	—	decreased
San Juan	increased	24–36	no	—	—
Seattle	—	5–24	yes	(f)	decreased
Trenton	same	6–12	no	—	decreased
Yonkers	increased	6	yes	20	decreased

Source: *The continued growth of hunger, homelessness and poverty in America's cities: 1986* (Washington, DC: United States Conference of Mayors, 1986), p. 32.

(a) Section 8: 10 years; Chicago Housing Authority: varies by development.
(b) Emergencies: 3 months.
(c) Normally: several years; emergencies: 3-6 months.
(d) Elderly: 1-3 months; families: 6 months.
(e) Public housing: 3 months; leased housing: 3 years.
(f) Families: 44 percent; elderly: 70 percent.

lem to the lack of ability to pay rent. Increasing the supply, preserving the existing supply, protesting tenant
rights and co-ordinating housing and community development are diminished concerns (p. 116).

DEINDUSTRIALIZATION

From the end of World War II through the late 1960s the
United States experienced an economic boom. The 1970s,
however, ushered in structural economic changes that altered
the nature of the U.S. economy and society. Known as "the
deindustrialization of America," the process has been transforming industry, the work force, and the structure of communities across the nation. During the 1970s at least 38 million
jobs in basic industry were permanently lost.

U.S. industry saw itself at a competitive disadvantage with
foreign industry because of its outmoded machinery and high
wages. The result was a decline in profits. The auto, steel,
rubber, and timber industries began enormous disinvestment
programs, resulting in numerous plant shutdowns and runaway shops. Jobs disappeared not only in the traditionally
industrialized Northeast, but also in many of the Sunbelt states.
As Bluestone and Harrison pointed out,

> None was more unprepared for such a shock than the
> state of California. . . . From South Gate to Hayward to
> Sacramento, across the state as a whole, in the single year
> 1980, at least 150 major plants closed their doors perma-
> nently, displacing more than 37,000 workers. The prob-
> lem has taken on epidemic proportions, affecting indus-
> tries as varied as automobile and trucks, rubber, steel,
> textiles, lumber, food processing and housewares (1982, p.
> 40).

Deindustrialization has affected minorities more than
whites. In a 1985 study by the U.S. Department of Labor entitled *Displaced Workers, 1979–83*, it was reported that between
1979 and 1983 a total of 11.5 million workers lost jobs because

of plant closings or employment cutbacks. This study then focused on the 5.1 million workers (of the 11.5 million displaced workers) who had worked at least three years on their jobs. Among this sample of 5.1 million displaced workers, the Department of Labor found that

> about 600,000 of the displaced workers were black and less than half of them were reemployed when interviewed (42 percent). Hispanic workers accounted for about 280,000 of the displaced. For them the proportion reemployed (52 percent) was higher than for Blacks but considerably lower than for Whites. Of the Whites who had been displaced, over three-fifths were reemployed and less than a quarter were unemployed (U.S. Department of Labor, 1985, p. 4; see Table 3.2.)

Deindustrialization results in much more economic displacement than is suffered directly by those affected by disinvestment in the company they work for. There is also the "ripple effect" of economic displacement. In a study of the consequences of the unemployment of 20,000 steelworkers in a two-county area of northwest Indiana in the early 1980s, researchers found that an additional 10,000 jobs were lost in the nonsteel sector of the local economy. When the unemployed steel workers started to cut back on the purchase of services and commodities, job loss resulted for many other types of workers in the community. Indeed, researchers projected that in a five-year period a total of 34,000 additional nonsteel jobs would be lost (Nyden, 1984, p. 9).

The "ripple effect" may partially explain why so many low-skilled service workers end up becoming homeless, in addition to the smaller, but no less significant, group of skilled blue collar workers, who sometimes become homeless after exhausting all their resources.

UNEMPLOYMENT

Deindustrialization has brought unprecedented unemployment, which continues at recession levels despite claims of

TABLE 3.2

Employment Status of Displaced Workers, by Age, Sex, Race, and Hispanic Origin, January 1984

Characteristic	Number (in thousands)[a]	Employed (%)	Unemployed (%)	Not in the Labor Force (%)
Age				
20-24 years	342	70.4	20.2	9.4
25-54 years	3,809	64.9	25.4	9.6
55-64 years	748	40.8	31.8	27.4
65 years and over	191	20.8	12.1	67.1
Total	5,091	60.1	25.5	14.4
Men				
20-24 years	204	72.2	21.7	6.1
25-54 years	2,570	68.2	26.8	5.0
55-64 years	461	43.6	34.1	22.3
65 years and over	92	16.8	12.9	70.3
Total	3,328	63.6	27.1	9.2
Women				
20-24 years	138	67.8	18.0	14.2
25-54 years	1,239	58.0	22.6	19.4
55-64 years	287	36.3	28.0	35.7
65 years and over	99	24.6	11.3	64.1
Total	1,763	53.4	22.5	24.2
White				
Men	2,913	66.1	25.1	8.8
Women	1,484	55.8	20.2	24.1
Total	4,397	62.6	23.4	13.9
Black				
Men	358	43.9	44.7	11.4
Women	244	38.8	35.6	25.6
Total	602	41.8	41.0	17.1
Hispanic origin				
Men	189	55.2	35.5	9.3
Women	93	46.3	30.0	23.6
Total	282	52.2	33.7	14.1

Source: *Displaced workers, 1979–83*. Bureau of Labor Statistics Bulletin 2240 (Washington, DC: U.S. Department of Labor, 1985), p. 20.

Note: Data for the race and hispanic-origin groups do not add up to totals because data for the "other races" group are not presented and because Hispanics are included in both the white and black population groups.

[a] Data refer to persons with tenure of 3 years or more who lost or left a job between January 1979 and January 1984 because of plant closings or moves, slack work, or the abolishment of their positions or shifts.

limited economic recovery. A probable indirect consequence has been the increase in homelessness, which nearly always begins with the kind of economic vulnerability produced by long-term unemployment.

The U.S. General Accounting Office report on the homeless states,

> In a survey of major southwest cities, 6 of the 7 ranked unemployment as the most important cause of homelessness, while all 10 cities included in the U.S. Conference of Mayors' study cited unemployment as a major cause of homelessness (1985, p. 9).

Between 1945 and 1975, the average national unemployment rate was 4.6 percent. By early 1984 it had more than doubled. The rise began after 1975 and reached a peak of 10.7 percent in November 1982, which followed the back-to-back recessions between 1979 and 1982. This was the highest unemployment rate since the Great Depression of the 1930s. The unduplicated count (no individual counted twice) of persons experiencing either unemployment, involuntary part-time employment, or low earnings (less than $6,700) in 1983 was 35.8 million (U.S. Department of Labor, 1985, p. 6). Although the official unemployment rate had dropped to 7.1 percent by June 1984, this figure represented 8,130,000 unemployed workers, 82,000 more people unemployed than when President Reagan took office in 1980. In fact, during Reagan's first three and one-half years in office, the average unemployment rate was 8.8 percent, and the average number of unemployed was 9,717,000, well above the average of any other president in U.S. history.

In addition to those included in the official unemployment rate, one must add discouraged workers who have stopped looking for work. Thus in June, 1984, when 8,130,000 people were officially unemployed, another 1.2 million were considered to have stopped looking. To these figures must be added the underemployed, the estimated 5.5 million who wanted full-time employment but were working part-time involuntarily (Belsie, 1986, p. 9).

TABLE 3.3
City Data on Economic Conditions

City	Population	Poverty 1986	Unemployment Situation, 1986	Unemployment Rate, September 1986	Projected Unemployment Situation, 1987	Economic Recovery Helped City?	Economic Recovery Helped Poor?
Boston	560,847	increased	same	5.3%	same	no	no
Charleston	69,510	increased	better	4.2	same	yes	no
Chicago	2,997,155	increased	same	8.7	worse	—	—
Cleveland	558,869	same	same	12.1	same	—	no
Denver	505,563	increased	worse	6.6	worse	no	no
Detroit	1,138,717	increased	—	11.1	worse	yes	no
Hartford	136,334	decreased	same	5.6	better	no	no
Kansas City	445,222	same	better	5.6	worse	yes	no
Los Angeles	3,022,247	increased	same	8.4	worse	yes	no
Louisville	293,531	increased	better	5.3	better	no	no

Minneapolis	369,161	increased	better	4.2	same	yes	yes
Nashville	455,252	increased	better	4.3	better	yes	yes
New Orleans	564,561	increased	worse	10.6	same	no	no
New York City	7,086,096	—	better	6.6	—	yes	no
Norfolk	266,874	same	same	4.0	same	yes	no
Philadelphia	1,665,382	—	better	6.2	better	yes	no
Phoenix	824,230	increased	same	5.9	same	no	no
Portland	367,530	increased	same	8.8	—	no	no
Salt Lake City	163,859	increased	same	5.5	same	yes	no
San Antonio	819,021	same	worse	8.2	—	no	no
San Francisco	691,637	increased	better	4.8	same	yes	no
San Juan	522,700	increased	worse	13.2*	worse	no	no
Seattle	490,077	increased	better	6.5	better	yes	no
Trenton	92,124	same	same	6.6	same	yes	no
Yonkers	192,342	decreased	better	4.2	better	yes	no

Source: Adapted from *The continued growth of hunger, homelessness, and poverty in America's cities: 1986* (Washington, DC: United States Conference of Mayors; 1986), pp. 42, 54.

*Unemployment rate is for metropolitan area.

These are national averages, which mask the impact of unemployment on specific regions and categories of people. Many local areas, of course, have been hit much harder. In Los Angeles County, for example, the July 1984 unemployment rate was 9.5 percent, significantly higher than the 7.5 percent national average.

The average unemployment rate for 1985 was 7.1 percent; for 1986 it was 7 percent. During 1985 only one out of three unemployed received unemployment benefits. This was the lowest percentage in the benefit program's history.

The 1986 United States Mayors Conference survey of 25 cities found that 58 percent of the cities reported that the unemployment situation had remained the same from the previous year or had gotten worse. (See Table 3.3.) However, in many of the cities that indicated an improved employment rate, the improvement was attributed to increases in individuals taking "part-time jobs at less than prevailing wages" and increases in the number of discouraged workers (1986b, pp. 37–38). When asked about the probable unemployment situation for 1987, of the cities that responded, 73 percent indicated that the unemployment situation would remain the same or worsen.

Of the cities surveyed, 61 percent believed the "economic recovery" had improved the "business climate," but 88 percent thought this economic recovery had not trickled down to help the poor and homeless (1986b, p. 39).

BLACK UNEMPLOYMENT

Annual average employment in Los Angeles County declined in both 1981 and 1983, for the first time since before World War II. The California Employment Development Department (CEDD) pointed to the recession of the early 1980s as "probably the most severe, in terms of its impact on unemployment . . . [of] any recession since the immediate post-war period" (California, 1984, p. 11).

The highest recorded monthly unemployment rate (11.5 percent) for Los Angeles was reached in February 1983, and during 1983 the average unemployment rate was 9.7 percent. (See Table 3.4.) If "discouraged workers" (unemployed who have given up looking for work because they cannot find jobs) are included, however, the average 1983 unemployment figure for Los Angeles County goes up to 13.6 percent.

As indicated in Table 3.5, the 1983 unemployment rate for Los Angeles was 16.4 percent for Blacks, 12.4 percent for Hispanics, and 9 percent for whites.

David Swinton, in his review of the economic status of Blacks in 1985, summarized the state of Black unemployment nationally in the following statement:

> Black unemployment reached record levels for the post WWII period during the recent recession. Thus, this latest recession continues the trend of each recession having a more devastating effect on the black population. Moreover, black unemployment rates were already high at the onset of the recession at 12.3% in 1979. The recession pushed the average black unemployment to 19.5% in 1983 even though the recovery phase had already begun. Since 1975, the annual average black unemployment rate has

TABLE 3.4

Los Angeles County Quarterly and Annual Unemployment Rates, 1974–1983

Year	Quarter 1	Quarter 2	Quarter 3	Quarter 4	Annual Average
1974	6.8	6.0	6.8	7.4	6.8
1975	10.3	9.9	9.6	9.0	9.7
1976	9.3	8.0	9.1	9.0	8.8
1977	8.7	7.6	8.3	7.3	8.0
1978	7.8	7.4	6.5	5.8	6.8
1979	6.1	5.2	5.9	4.8	5.5
1980	5.6	6.4	7.1	7.1	6.6
1981	6.9	6.5	6.9	7.3	6.9
1982	8.6	8.6	9.6	10.4	9.3
1983	10.9	10.0	10.1	7.8	9.7

TABLE 3.5
Los Angeles County Annual Average Unemployment Rates,
for Worker Groups

	1981	1982	1983
Total	6.9	9.3	9.7
Men	7.1	9.4	10.7
Women	6.7	9.1	8.3
Both, 16–19 years	22.0	22.6	25.3
White	6.2	8.8	9.0
Men		9.0	9.9
Women		8.5	7.7
Both, 16–19 years		20.5	21.6
Black	13.7	14.2	16.4
Men		14.6	18.9
Women		13.7	13.6
Both, 16–19 years		39.6	50.5
Hispanic origin	9.2	12.8	12.4
Men	7.4	13.0	13.0
Women			
Both, 16–19 years	25.0	25.0	28.4
Single (never married)	13.8	14.8	
Married, spouse present	6.9	7.0	

Source: *Annual planning information, Los Angeles–Long Beach SMSA 1984–85.* (Sacramento, CA: California Department of Employment Development, 1984.)

been 15.2%. There has been no year during this period in which black unemployment was less than 12%. Since 1981 the black unemployment rates have averaged 17% and there hasn't been a single year in the last five when black unemployment was less than 15%. Even for the first three quarters of 1985, the third year of the recovery, black unemployment averaged 15.1% (1986, p. 14).

As the data in Chapter 1 demonstrate, approximately 20 percent of the homeless population, whether white, black, Hispanic or other, are working full or part time, and 50 percent of each group is actively looking for work. The data also indicate that the nonwhite homeless are unemployed longer than the white.

Economic reasons (no money, no job) were given by all groups (approximately 90 percent of each group) for their homelessness.

POVERTY AND WELFARE

Recession-level unemployment and underemployment have contributed to the rising poverty rate, and cutbacks in social welfare programs have added to the impact. The official poverty rate rose from 11.7 percent in 1979 (26.1 million poor Americans), to 15 percent in 1982 (34.4 million) and to 15.2 percent in 1983 (35.3 million), its highest level in 18 years—a family of four in 1983 was considered below the poverty line if its income was less than $10,178. In 1984, the number of Americans living below the poverty line (35.3 million) exceeded the number who were poor at the beginning of the "war on poverty" in 1965. The number of poor had increased by 6 million since 1980 (Cimons, 1983).

A different set of statistics shows who is poor in America. In 1983, 25 percent of children under six (5.3 million) were poor, as were 14.1 percent of people 65 and older, 35.7 percent of blacks, 28.4 percent of Hispanics, and 12 percent of whites. These percentages remained relatively the same in 1987. During this time, cuts in various welfare programs and tightening of eligibility criteria have exacerbated the already precarious economic and social plight of many low-income Americans. In the Social Security Disability insurance program alone, for example, the tightening of eligibility criteria led to the exclusion of 150,000 to 200,000 former recipients between March 1981 and April 1984 (Bassuk, 1984a).

Even public relief programs that are geared to providing aid to the homeless have sometimes proven haphazard and inadequate. Until mid-1984, for example, the County of Los Angeles required identification to establish eligibility for temporary vouchers, which could be exchanged for a room in a skid row hotel. Since the IDs of most homeless persons are either lost or stolen, this requirement rendered most of them ineligible for aid until the provision was suspended as a result of a lawsuit.

General relief recipients may be denied welfare funds for 60 days for missing or being late for appointments, or for failing to fill out forms correctly. It is estimated that some 3,000 persons per month in Los Angeles become homeless when they are eliminated from the general relief program by the "60-day penalty." A 1984 study by the Los Angeles County Department of Public Social Services found that the typical male employable recipient of general relief is a 37-year-old black male who "most likely turned to general relief due to lay-off or expiration of unemployment benefits" (Los Angeles County, 1983).

All the factors mentioned thus far have contributed to maintaining the gap between the rich and the poor in America. In 1983 those at the top one-fifth of U.S. income distribution averaged nine times more income than the bottom fifth; a decade earlier the ratio was seven to one. At the same time, the poorest one-fifth of American families experienced a decrease in their share of income from 5.5 percent in 1974 to 4.7 percent in 1983.

Many Americans like to think of themselves as middle-class people, but in the 1980s economic and social forces are producing a "bipolar" society characterized by a shrinking middle class. The result is a polarized class structure. Between 1968 and 1983, the percentage of the U.S. population defined as middle class (based on relation to the median income of the population) declined. It is believed that the "globalization" of the economy that has resulted from disinvestment in U.S. industries drives down U.S. wages, and the newly created "service" jobs pay far less than industrial production jobs. For example, in 1984 the average weekly wage of the 14 million workers in service industries was $206.67, while that of the 13 million workers in "precision production" jobs averaged $275.65 per week (Persell, 1987, p. 212).

Today, most of the poor live in metropolitan areas. In the

central cities of these areas the poverty rate has increased from 14.9 percent in 1970 to 18 percent in 1982. Black families, whether male- or female-headed, are overrepresented among the urban poor. John Jacob, in his overview of black America in 1985, summarized black poverty with the following statement:

> The overall black poverty rate in 1984 was 33.8%, down from 35.7% in 1983, but higher than the black poverty rate for any non-recession year since 1968.
>
> Most of the decline in black poverty occurred among the elderly. The black elderly poverty rate fell from 36.2% to 31.7%. This drop was due in part to increases in Social Security and Supplemental Security income benefits (1986, p. 1).

INCREASE IN FAMILY INSTABILITY

Family instability and domestic violence often lead to the temporary homelessness of spouses and other family members. The rate of divorce is now one-half the marriage rate, and some form of domestic violence occurs in every sixth household in U.S. cities. Tens of thousands of young people flee their homes annually to escape mental and physical abuse. In New York City alone, it is estimated that 3,700 youth seek shelter each year. Domestic violence also forces thousands of women to leave their homes. The precarious economic circumstances of many American families compound family instability, often resulting in greater drug and alcohol abuse, abandonment, and increased domestic violence (Ropers & Marks, 1983). The number of female-headed families below the poverty line in 1982 was dramatically higher than in 1970, and the number of white and black female-headed families has doubled since 1970. In 1982, 67 percent of the 2.4 million central city poverty families were headed by women. In 1985, 53.1 percent of Hispanic families headed by women and 50.5 percent of black families headed by women lived below the poverty level. The median income for Hispanic families was $19,027, for black families, $16,786, and for white families $29,152 ("Hispanic poverty rate," 1986).

The state of black families is summarized in this statement by researcher David Swinton:

> The differences between black and white family structures also intensified during the past few years. In 1984 there were almost 33 percentage points fewer black married couple families than white—52% of black families were married couples versus 84.9% of white. The absolute gap between the proportion of black and white married couple families increased from 31.5 percentage points in 1980 to 32.9 percentage points in 1984. Blacks had almost three and one half times as large a percentage of female-headed families in 1984 than did whites (44.4% v. 12.9%) and about one and a half times as large a proportion of male-headed families—5.2% v. 3.4%. Thus the relatively disadvantageous family status distribution of black families has intensified in the last few years (1986, p. 5).

DEINSTITUTIONALIZATION OF MENTAL PATIENTS

Large numbers of mental patients in the United States have been "deinstitutionalized." Between 1955 and 1983 the total was 433,722. The process was precipitated by (a) the introduction of tranquilizing phenothiazine drugs, (b) establishment of community mental health centers, (c) critiques of mental hospitals as inhuman, prison-like storehouses for the mentally ill, and (d) cutbacks in federal and state funding.

Dr. Alan Leavitt, program chief of Community Mental Health Services in San Francisco, has estimated that an additional 55,000 persons in California would be in psychiatric institutions if the criteria used in 1960 were applied in 1983. Of that number, he believes 38,000 are currently in nursing homes or board and care homes. Another 12,000 are living independently with some treatment, while the remaining 5,000 may be untreated and essentially homeless (Waters, 1984).

Deinstitutionalization has undoubtedly contributed to the

homeless population, and the homeless mentally ill are often the most highly visible of the homeless. On the other hand, their proportion is less than some claim. The HUD report on homelessness concluded, "If deinstitutionalization is defined narrowly as the release of long-term residents of mental institutions, its effect (on the homeless problem) has been minor" (HUD, 1984, p. 24). In the most comprehensive studies to date on the relationships among deinstitutionalization, mental illness, and homelessness, the Ohio Department of Mental Health recently completed a study of 1,000 homeless persons and a study of discharged mental patients from state hospitals. The department found that only 6 percent of their 1,000 homeless respondents had been hospitalized during the period (1960–1980) when Ohio had a dramatic decline in its state mental hospital population. In the study of discharged patients in fiscal year 1982–1983, they found only 4 percent to be homeless. The Ohio study concludes, "It is again the case that study findings stand in contrast to current views about homeless people. The idea that most homeless people are mentally ill and in need of mental hospitalization is not supported by the data" (Ohio, 1985).

New York State Governor Mario Cuomo's report to the National Governors Association Task Force on the Homeless concluded,

> Lest there be any misunderstanding, the bulk of research to date indicates that (1) the majority of the homeless poor are not seriously mentally disabled; and that (2) even for those with severe disabilities, preferable alternatives to re-hospitalization exist, although in far too short a supply. Moreover, it is often not a simple matter to judge to what degree an observed disorder should be considered a cause, and to what degree a consequence of street-living (1983, p. 42).

While it is undoubtedly true that most homeless persons suffer from the psychological distress of being homeless, empirical studies have demonstrated that only a minority of the homeless are deinstitutionalized chronic mental patients or are currently suffering from a chronic mental illness that causes them to be homeless (Ohio, 1985; Fischer & Breakey, 1986; Ropers & Boyer, 1987a).

It is important to distinguish having a "lifetime prevalence" for hospitalization or mental illness from being a recently deinstitutionalized long-term patient or being currently "mentally ill." The majority (66 percent) of the homeless respondents in the Los Angeles sample described in Chapter 1 had never been hospitalized for drug, alcohol, or psychiatric problems. And of those who had been hospitalized, only 15 percent indicated a lifetime prevalence of hospitalization for purely psychiatric reasons. Unfortunately, in the view of many health professionals and the lay public, the term "homeless" has too often come to mean mentally ill.

REAGAN'S "GRATE" SOCIETY: POLITICAL POLICIES THAT CONTRIBUTE TO HOMELESSNESS

> One problem we've had, even in the best of times . . . is the people who are sleeping on the grates, the homeless who are homeless, you might say, by choice (Ronald Reagan, quoted in "Homeless by choice?," 1984).

The long-term social and economic transformations discussed up to this point were obviously not the product or responsibility of the Reagan administration. But there can be no doubt that the domestic policies of this administration have greatly exacerbated the effects of long-term social and economic trends. Political perspectives on the homeless crisis are clearly partisan, and it is no coincidence that the dramatic increase in the homeless population has occurred primarily during Reagan's tenure.

Reagan's former Secretary of Health and Human Services, Margaret Heckler, summarized the White House view of the causes of homelessness when she stated,

> The problem of homelessness is not a new problem. It is correlated to the problem of alcohol or drug dependency.

And there have been a number of alcoholics who become homeless throughout the years, maybe centuries. They are still there. . . . I see the mentally handicapped as the latest group of the homeless. But, the problem is as old as time and with this new dimension complicating it, it's a serious problem, but it always has been (quoted in Hopper & Hamberg, 1986, p. 33).

By failing to acknowledge the national long-term structural causes of homelessness and instead placing the blame on the presumed characteristics of the homeless, the Reagan administration has been able to contend that homelessness is a problem that transcends politics and national trends. Consequently, the Reagan administration maintains that the causes of homelessness are situated in personal pathologies, which should be addressed by local communities.

In 1983, the Department of Health and Human Services (HHS) created a Federal Interagency Task Force on Homelessness, which proceeded on the assumptions that homelessness is essentially a local problem and that new federal programs for the homeless are not the answer. Basically, the task force attempted to serve as a broker between the federal government and private-sector agencies seeking assistance in aiding the homeless (GAO, 1985, pp. 34–45).

In 1985 the federal role in aiding the homeless was limited to two appropriations. One was for $70 million to purchase food and provide shelter for the poor and homeless. The funds were distributed through the Federal Emergency Management Agency (FEMA) to state and local public agencies. FEMA did not ask for any additional funds for fiscal year 1986. With the other appropriation HHS provided up to $5 million for the establishment of a 1,000-bed model shelter in Washington, DC.

The continued and dramatic increases in the size of the homeless population and the large number of families with children (28 percent) who are homeless, plus the continued pressure from advocates for the homeless and Democratic Party congress members, finally motivated President Reagan, on July 22, 1987, to sign a $1 billion emergency bill for the homeless. The new law allows Congress to spend $425 million in fiscal year 1987 and $617 million in fiscal year 1988 (Safety Network, 1987, p. 1).

The Reagan administration domestic policies, however, have clearly had a negative impact on the poor and homeless, specifically in the areas of housing, national economic policy, and social welfare. The administration approach to low-income housing has been dominated by a "free market" policy. The Reagan administration came into power determined to cut back on the $30 billion the government was spending on low-income housing. By 1983 the administration had introduced housing-subsidy vouchers which could be used by low-income families to find housing on their own at whatever price they could negotiate. This program has had limited success. In New York City, for example, 200,000 low-income families are on a waiting list for low-income housing, and 62 percent of the families that were offered vouchers had to return them unused. Despite federal assistance, these families had not been able to find decent and affordable housing in New York's closed housing market ("Freedom of choice," 1987).

Since 1980 there has been a dramatic drop in all government low-income housing starts, including all public housing programs, Section 8 construction and rehabilitation, and Section 202 housing for the elderly and handicapped. Government housing starts for these programs numbered 183,000 units for 1980 but only 28,000 for 1985 (Hartman, 1986, p. 364).

Under the Reagan administration, the Department of Housing and Urban Development (HUD), headed by Samuel Pierce, has been subject to some of the most severe budget cuts of any Reagan cabinet department. Its budget has gone from $35.7 billion in fiscal 1980 to $14.2 billion in fiscal 1987, and the number of households targeted for new housing aid in 1987 is about 74,000, compared with 192,000 in 1980. By the year 2000 about 33 percent of all households and 70 percent of low-income households are expected to face problems of housing adequacy or affordability (Riordan, 1987). The tragedy is that it will take years to undo the damage, even if a different administration has the motivation.

Unemployment Compensation

In March 1985 the Reagan administration and the U.S. Congress decided not to keep the Federal Supplemental Compensation program, which had enabled unemployed workers who qualified to receive additional unemployment compensation for an extra 8 to 14 weeks. About 340,000 unemployed workers lost their benefits when the program was terminated.

Normally, qualified unemployed workers receive 26 weeks of unemployment compensation, but in 1985 fewer than one of three unemployed workers received this compensation. This was the lowest percentage in the program's history.

The Reagan administration argued that "economic recovery" was creating new jobs and that job training should replace programs such as Federal Supplemental Compensation. Administration officials also suggested that the unemployed should move, and go to the "South and the West," where the new jobs were going (May, 1985).

Low-Income Programs

Every year since it has been in office, the Reagan administration has proposed numerous cuts and terminations of assistance programs for poor Americans. Although Congress has modified or denied many of the proposed program cuts, in many areas the administration has been successful. Programs directed at low-income families make up less than one-tenth of the federal budget, but have been cut $57 billion in just the 1981–1985 period (Center on Budget and Policy Priorities, 1984, p. 2). Between fiscal 1982 and 1985, $7 billion was cut from the food-stamp program. In 1982 the federal subsidy of school lunch programs was substantially cut back and eligibility criteria made more restrictive. About $5 billion was cut from child nutrition programs between 1982 and 1985 (Brown, 1987, p. 41).

According to some authorities, these cuts have resulted in increased hunger and infant mortality. Hunger has been defined as being "chronically short of the nutrients necessary for growth and good health" (Brown, 1987, p. 37).

The U.S. infant mortality rate is currently 11.2, which

TABLE 3.6
Reductions Enacted in Selected Low-Income Programs*
(in %)

Program	Reduction
Food stamps	− 13.8
Child nutrition	− 28.0
AFDC	− 14.3
Housing assistance	− 11.4
Low-income energy assistance	− 8.3
Medicaid	− 2.8
Public service employment	− 100.0
Unemployment insurance	− 17.4

Source: Adapted from *End results: The impact of federal policies on low-income Americans*, (Washington, DC: Center on Budget and Policy Priorities, 1984), pp. 8–9.

places the United States eighteenth-lowest in the world. The situation for nonwhite infants is even worse and exceeds the infant mortality rate of Cuba and Jamaica (Brown, 1987, pp. 38–39).

There have been substantial cuts in Aid to Families with Dependent Children (AFDC), with at least 500,000 low-income families terminated. At least 40 states have made cuts in Medicaid, the program that provides basic medical coverage for low-income families (Center on Budget and Policy Priorities, 1984, p. 3). The actual program cuts enacted in various low-income programs as of fiscal 1985 are summarized in Table 3.6.

Reagan's proposed budget cuts for fiscal 1988 continued the attack on low-income programs. Targeted once again were food stamps and school lunches, Medicaid, Home Energy Assistance, and the Work Incentives program. In addition, HUD appropriations were slashed about 70 percent between 1981 and 1987, and Reagan was expected to try to cut appropriations back even more in 1988 ("Homeless aid gets boost," 1987).

Altogether, Reagan called for $9 billion in cuts in health, welfare, and other social service programs for 1988. The Congress, dominated by members of the Democratic Party, was expected to modify many of the proposed cuts, however.

Chapter 4

THEORETICAL APPROACHES

From Blaming the Victim to Social Disaffiliation and Displacement

A host of theories and models attempt to account for the processes by which individuals become homeless. In the previous literature they range from psychiatric medical models to sociological structural theories. The literature that appeared before the 1980s dealt primarily with the skid row homeless male population, with most explanations focusing on the defects and shortcomings of the subjects.

In addition to individual vulnerabilities to personal and social crises, the recent dramatic increases in the homeless population and its diversity suggest that theories must consider the large-scale economic and social trends producing homelessness in the 1980s.

The previous contributions of H. Bahr and T. Caplow (1974) and Bogue (1963) are still useful as a partial basis for formulating a model of homelessness in the 1980s. Bahr and Caplow suggested that the concept of "social disaffiliation" (p. 55) may be the "unifying element" for different types of homeless persons. Whatever the origin of an individual's homelessness, the result is some degree of detachment from mainstream social roles, institutions, and structure. It is this detachment to which the concept of "disaffiliation" refers. Disaffiliation is by no means limited to an individualistic view of the origins of homelessness; detachment from social roles and institutions may be imposed on individuals through various forms of social, economic, and political displacement, as well as the idiosyncratic aspects of their personal lives.

Three major paths to social disaffiliation have been identified by Bahr and Caplow:

1. External changes may leave individuals with few affiliations.
2. The individual may estrange himself from society.
3. A handicap may lead to lifetime isolation (1974, pp. 56–67).

External changes beyond the immediate control of the individuals may leave them with few affiliations. As Bahr and Caplow have stated, "society may be seen as withdrawing from the individual; his world disappears, and he remains alone and unattached, a stranger from another time or place" (1974, pp. 56–57).

The most dramatic external social changes are often socio-economic changes, such as economic depressions and recessions or technological innovations that result in job displacement. Wars, revolutions, and other major political changes may also eliminate jobs or cause the deaths of family members. Natural catastrophes such as floods, fires, and earthquakes may have the same effects. Illness and old age are also beyond the control of individuals and may make them unable to function in their social roles.

A second path to disaffiliation is individual estrangement from social roles and organizations. Individuals who "freely" choose to deviate from social norms may find themselves stigmatized, outlawed, and even exiled from mainstream society. Included in this category might be drug and alcohol addicts, criminals, and political dissenters.

The third path to disaffiliation involves what Bahr and Caplow describe as "unsocialization" leading to "lifetime isolation" (1974, p. 57). The chronically mentally ill, the mentally retarded, and the physically disabled might be included in this group.

Whatever path leads an individual to disaffiliation, the end result may be the extreme of long-term, episodic, or transitional homelessness. As the disaffiliation process becomes complete, individuals may find themselves cut off from all social, psychological, institutional, and material supports.

JOB DISPLACEMENT AND THE DISAFFILIATION OF UNEMPLOYMENT

The relatively high unemployment rates of the 1980s are largely the result of the deindustrialization of American industry, a process well beyond the control of the individual worker. The economic and social displacement resulting from unemployment, in addition to being one of the primary precipitants of homelessness, has numerous and well-documented social, physical, and psychological consequences for the individual.

In addition to severing the individual from the main source of material existence for most people—income—unemployment detaches the worker from a pivotal social role—work. That is, a job provides not only income, but also self-esteem and a patterned activity that shapes other life activities. Unemployment disaffiliates the worker from some of society's most important social and economic institutions.

Through the disaffiliation caused by economic displacement, we may begin to understand not only how homeless individuals become detached from the job and housing markets, but also how they begin to become estranged socially and psychologically. Homelessness is an unfortunate continuation of the displacement process that begins with the social and psychological disaffiliation from unemployment.

The court testimony of an unemployed cabinet worker from Tucson, who came to Los Angeles in 1984 to find work but instead found himself and his wife homeless in the "city of angels," illustrates the relationship between unemployment and homelessness.

I am 36 years old. I am homeless. I came to Los Angeles with my wife from Tucson, Arizona. I came to find work.

On the same day we came to Los Angeles, we were robbed at knife point by four guys. They took all our money ($112.00) and my identification. They took all my clothes, except what I have on.

Since being robbed, we have been living on the streets. My wife is still terrified from being robbed. So we walk around all night. When we can't go on, we stop and sit down and get a little sleep. I watch over my wife while she sleeps. I don't sleep much myself. We were last in a bed over a week ago.

A minister told me we could get help at the welfare office. The welfare worker told me all they could do was give us each a check for $8.00. They did not give us any food stamps or money for food.

We had last eaten at a mission on May 7. We had nothing at all to eat on May 8. We looked for a hotel room. We went in 15 or 16 hotels. None of them had a room for $16.00 for two people. I tried all the places in skid row. None of them had a room we could afford. Finally, we gave up looking for a place about 2:00 a.m., after walking around since 5:30 p.m. Neither of us had eaten for more than 36 hours. We spent some of the money on food, after it become clear we were never going to find a place.

We then began walking the streets again, as we have done for the past week. As long as you keep moving, the police don't bother you. But we try to stay in well lighted areas so we don't get attacked again. But when we stop, the cops make us move on.

The hardest thing has been having to watch my wife suffer through this. She isn't as tough as I am. She has really changed in the last week. She is nervous and de-pressed all the time.

We don't need much. We don't want to do wrong. We only want to survive. But we have to have a place to stay. I'm not going to leave my wife alone while I look for work.

> She is too scared of being attacked again. Not that I can
> look for work anyway. I haven't had a shower in a week.
>   We have never been on welfare. I last worked as a
> cabinet maker in Tucson. I want to work. There just isn't
> any work. For now I just have to sit here with my wife,
> waiting to see what will happen (Ross, 1984).

The negative effects of unemployment reported from numerous studies have indicated significant increments in depression, anxiety, and psychiatric morbidity and substantial decrements in life satisfaction and self-esteem (Ware, Davis-Avery, & Donald, 1978; Dooley & Catalano, 1980; Ropers & Scott, 1980). Several studies have noted the connection between unemployment/economic factors and suicide (Lendrum, 1933; Salinsbury, 1956; Tuckman & Lavell, 1958; Breed, 1963; MacMahon, Johnson, & Pugh, 1963; Pierce, 1967; Theorell, Lind, & Floderus, 1975; Brenner, 1973; Vigderhous & Fishman, 1978).

Of all the problems facing working individuals, unemployment and its debilitating physical, psychological, social, and economic effects is perhaps one of the most serious. As several researchers have pointed out (Eisenberg & Lazarsfeld 1938; Komarovsky 1940, 81; Tiffany, Cowan, & Tiffany 1970, 62; Wilcock & Franke 1963, 91; Braginsky & Braginsky 1975), a person's job is an important source of a person's self-esteem in the American culture and often provides the sole or primary organizing basis for an individual's social behavior and attitudes. Unemployment may have a shattering effect on an individual's self-esteem, consequently increasing the possibility of personality and behavioral problems (Braginsky & Braginsky 1975).

Of the many social roles an individual plays and takes daily, the work role often sets the parameters of other roles in terms of opportunity, time, interest, and resources. Unemployment leaves the individual without the central organizing function of the work role. Given the dominant cultural values of our economic and social system, wherein the male is still often the central "breadwinner" of a family, unemployment is

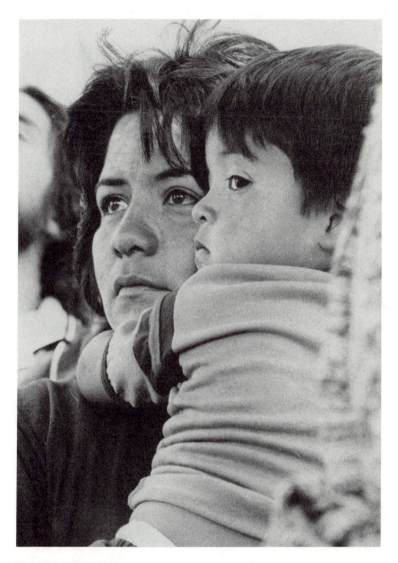

Families with children make up one-third of the homeless. Photo by Mary Ann Dolcemascolo.

Ted Hayes, organizer of the homeless. Photo by Mary Ann Dolce-mascolo.

Author with organizer of the Los Angeles homeless Ted Hayes, May 1987. Photo by Mona Lee Harris.

Out, but not down. Photo by Mary Ann Dolcemascolo.

Third-world living in downtown Los Angeles. Photo by Mona Lee Harris.

SRO living: Out of sight, out of mind. Photo by Mary Ann Dolce-mascolo.

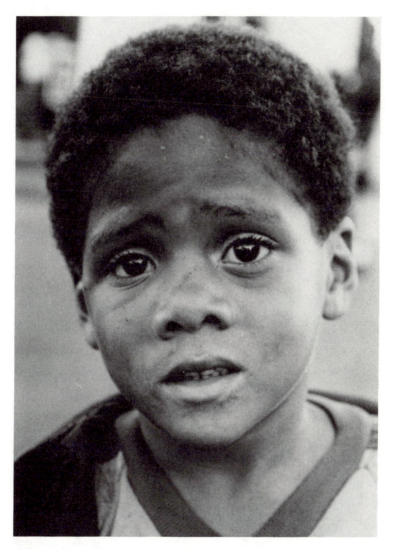

Child of the street: homeless by choice? Photo by Mary Ann Dolce-mascolo.

Harry Rodgers, organizer of the homeless, who was stabbed to death in 1985 while attempting to break up a fight in a soup kitchen line. Photo by Mary Ann Dolcemascolo.

Homeless living in Los Angeles. Photo by Mary Ann Dolcemascolo.

They have taken everything but our pride. Photo by Mary Ann Dolce-mascolo.

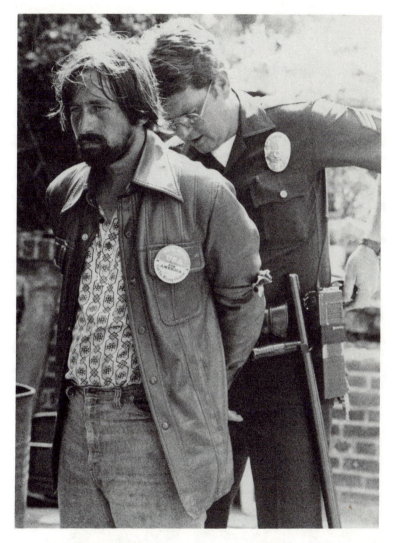
Justice at "Justiceville"—charge: trespassing. Photo by Mary Ann Dolcemascolo.

Young, black, unemployed, and homeless. Photo by Mary Ann Dolcemascolo.

especially destructive to the self-esteem of a man. As Mirra Komarovsky has pointed out,

> For most of the men in our culture, work is apparently the sole organizing principle and the only means of self-expression. The other interests, personal and social relations—turned out to be too weak and insignificant for their personalities to furnish any meaning to their lives (1940, p. 81).

The loss of a socially meaningful role such as the work role can weaken the social identity and self-esteem of any individual, male or female, single or married, young or old. Unemployment disrupts the established role sets of individuals and has serious consequences for the frames of reference that orient an individual's identity and social interactions with family and peers and in other social situations.

As a report of a Special Task Force to the Secretary of Health, Education, and Welfare states,

> The tension generated by chronic money shortages is raised to even higher levels if the husband also experiences intermittent or prolonged unemployment. There is always the question in everyone's mind that his being unemployed may be "his own fault." He is "surplus man" around the house because the sharp division of labor in the lower-class family gives him a minimally active role in housekeeping and child rearing, and because the wife feels he should be out working or looking for work. And since unemployment in low-income households is often a reality and always a prospect—or even if he works steadily, he may not be bringing home enough to live on—the man is constantly vulnerable to the definition, his own or others' or both, that something is wrong with him, that he does not want to work, or if he is working that he is simply not worth enough to be paid a living wage (HEW, 1973, pp. 182–183).

Additionally, as Frank Furstenburg points out, after reviewing 46 studies relating work experience and family life, "economic uncertainty brought on by unemployment is a principal reason why family relations deteriorate" (as quoted in HEW, 1973).

The loss of the work role and all that it grants—income, self-identity, social integration, and so on—is bound to influence, if not disrupt, individual and family stability. Often the disruption of occupational or career goals can result in a failure to fulfill marital expectations about the "good life," the "happy home," or the "meaningful life." The work role is undoubtedly a pivotal social role around which all family roles and expectations revolve. Job demands and requirements often set the parameters of individual and family routines and schedules. Loss of a job means the loss of an essential integrative tie to society for the individual. Unemployment often means a separation from coworkers, many of whom may have been among the individual's good friends. Since most workers are "paying off" their mortgages, cars, TVs, and other appliances, unemployment simply aggravates an already precarious situation. Unfortunately, the frustration and anxiety produced by loss of one's job may also have disastrous consequences for the children in the family. Some studies have shown that child abuse is much more prevalent among the unemployed than the employed (*Federationist*, 1979, p. 24).

Regarding the effects of unemployment on the family, in a 1976 study for the Joint Economic Committee of Congress, Harvey Brenner of Johns Hopkins University put it this way:

> In the case of the family, substantial changes may be necessary in its pattern of functioning and in its lifestyle. It is possible for patterns of relationship in the family, including relations between husband and wife, to change and also for patterns of authority, governing relations between parents and children, to be altered. The intra-familial problems could either stem from the agitation of several of the family members over the loss of income and social position, or from the sense of failure that might be held by the person who becomes unemployed and is felt to initiate the family's problems. Due to a decline in family

resources or a general sense of shame, it is possible for community relationships and friendship patterns to suffer as a result of decreased contact (1976, p. 92–93).

Aside from the need for a family or individual to adjust to a lower income, to readjust routines and expectations because of unemployment, there is the problem of psychological stress and lower self-esteem, which may have serious consequences for unemployed individuals and their relationships with others.

The relationship between unemployment and likely indicators of psychological stress is well established. To quote Brenner again,

> A one percent increase in the unemployment rate sustained over a period of six years has been associated (during the past three decades) with increases of approximately:
> —36,887 deaths, including 20,240 cardiovascular deaths;
> —920 suicides;
> —648 homicides;
> —495 deaths from cirrhosis of the liver;
> —4,227 state mental hospital admissions; and
> —3,340 state prison admissions (1976, pp. 5–6).

In 1983, as a UCLA postdoctoral intern at a community mental health center in Los Angeles, the author was a facilitator and researcher for a crisis intervention group for the unemployed.

The unemployed clients ($n = 42$) in this crisis intervention group were asked to indicate, among a select list of life events, which life events had happened to them six months prior to becoming unemployed and which after they became unemployed. They were also asked to indicate what types of problems had occurred as a result of their unemployment.

Of the group, 60 percent reported one or more life events since being unemployed. The group reported only seven life events occurring six months before becoming unemployed, compared with 65 life events after becoming unemployed. Table 4.1 gives the percentages of participants who experi-

TABLE 4.1
Unemployment and Selected Life Events
(in percentage)

	Six Months Before Becoming Unemployed	*After Becoming Unemployed*
Death of spouse	0	2.4
Marital separation	2.4	7.1
Got married	0	0
Increased alcohol abuse	0	16.6
Increased drug abuse	0	12.0
Birth of a child in immediate family	0	0
Violence in family	2.4	9.5
Was arrested	0	2.4
Made suicide attempt	2.4	2.4
Talked to someone about suicide	2.4	19.0
Loss or change of home/residence	0	21.0
Illness	2.4	14.0
Death of close friend	0	0
New person living in household	0	5.0
Divorce	0	5.0
Broken engagement or broken love relationship	5.0	12.0
Increased problems with children	0	26.0

$\overline{X}$ length of unemployment   = 37 weeks
Median length unemployment = 24.5 weeks

enced different selected life events before and after becoming unemployed. Change or loss of residence (21 percent), increased alcohol abuse (16.5 percent), talking about suicide (19 percent), illness (14 percent), and increased problems with children (26 percent) were the leading events experienced since becoming unemployed.

In response to other questions, 55 percent of the participants indicated that family arguments had increased since unemployment, and 29 percent indicated that their health was worse since being unemployed. Fifty-five percent blamed their unemployment on the crisis of the economy.

Table 4.2 indicates by percentage the reasons given by participants for entering this crisis intervention program for the unemployed. Depression (55 percent) and anxiety (52 percent) were the leading motivators, followed by family problems (29 percent).

Psychiatrist Richard Warner, in his comprehensive study of the relation between schizophrenia and the economy, concluded,

> Indeed, the similarity of many features of chronic schizophrenia to the psychological effects of extended unemployment is striking. Anxiety, depression, apathy, irritability, negativity, emotional overdependence, social withdrawal, isolation and loneliness, and a loss of self-respect, identity and a sense of time—all these are common amongst the long-term unemployed (1985, p. 133).

Clearly, since the vast majority of homeless individuals have come to be homeless because of their unemployment or underemployment, their psychological condition is probably in large measure a result of the psychosocial stresses of unem-

TABLE 4.2
Types of Problems Reported Since Unemployed
(in percentage)

Family problems	29.0
Marital problems	17.0
Depression	55.0
Anxiety	52.0
Relations with children	19.0
Health-related problems	9.5
Other	19.0

ployment, compounded by the lack of a home. Undoubtedly, the social and economic displacement caused by unemployment can and does often result in various forms of psychological and social disaffiliation.

A great deal has been written by psychiatrists about the mentally ill and drug and alcohol addicts among the homeless. Bahr and Caplow would count these groups as on the "estrangement" and "lifetime isolation" paths to disaffiliation. An examination of the extent to which estrangement and isolation contribute to the new urban homeless populations of the 1980s is in order.

THE PSYCHIATRIC PRACTICE OF BLAMING THE VICTIM

Psychologist William Ryan, in his classic book *Blaming the Victim*, has argued that a process of evasion dominates thought about social problems in the United States. The evasion Ryan writes about is the distraction of attention away from the structural causes of social problems, a process that he claims leaves "primary social injustice untouched" (1971, p. 25).

In place of explaining social problems in terms of their social origins, explanations that focus and dwell on the characteristics and attributes of those injured by unfortunate circumstances beyond their control are offered as the reasons for social problems. It is this process of inversion of cause and effect which Ryan calls the "blaming the victim ideology."

Ryan describes the basic steps of the process of blaming the victim in the following way:

> All of this happens so smoothly that it seems downright rational. First, identify a social problem. Second, study those affected by the problem and discover in what ways they are different from the rest of us as a consequence of deprivation and injustice. Third, define the differences as the cause of the social problem itself. Finally, of course, assign a government bureaucrat to invent a humanitarian action program to correct the differences (1971, pp. 8–9).

For Ryan, the blaming-the-victim approach is not simply one among many theoretical explanations for social problems; instead, it is an ideological process that can "take its place in a long series of American ideologies that have rationalized cruelty and injustice" (1971, p. 20).

Every social problem, including crime, delinquency, unemployment, poverty, civil disorder, mental illness and now homelessness has been and continues to be analyzed through blaming-the-victim approaches. The professionals, liberal or conservative, who are in the business of treating, managing, and controlling the victims of social problems sometimes unwittingly become ideologues of the blaming-the-victim perspective. Becoming an ideologue is a result of a compromise between their self-interest and genuine humanitarian concerns. They can avoid criticism of current social conditions and arrangements from which they may benefit personally while at the same time believing they are acting in a charitable fashion by aiding individuals who are somehow afflicted with a social, physical, or mental pathology.

It is regrettable that blaming-the-victim interpretations of homelessness have dominated the professional literature, particularly psychiatric discussions, during the past several years.

There is no question that most of the homeless suffer from the psychosocial stress produced by their state of unemployment and lack of a home. The empirical evidence of Chapter 1 clearly demonstrates that demoralization is a leading psychological affliction of the homeless.

There can also be no doubt that some among the homeless are suffering from chronic and serious forms of mental illness. The clinical experience of numerous mental health professionals testifies to that fact. In no way should the existence and needs of the homeless mentally ill be dismissed.

Nevertheless, there are other issues regarding the prevalence and incidence of mental illness among the homeless that unfortunately seem to be complicated by political, professional, personal, and even ideological self-interest. When the claims of some segments of the mental health profession regarding the prevalence of mental illness among the homeless are examined, these claims often appear to be scientifically vacuous. If the contentions that homelessness is caused by deinstitutionalization or that homelessness is itself a symptom of mental illness and that nearly half or more of the homeless are mentally ill can be demonstrated not to be supported by scientific evidence, then perhaps such assertions are ideological in nature.

A number of psychiatrists have played a key role by offering various theories and explanations for the rise of the new urban homeless, theories and explanations that have captured the attention of the mass media and influenced public perception of the problem. Often psychiatrists claim that the deinstitutionalization of mental patients is the leading or primary cause of homelessness, that most of the homeless have a chronic mental illness, and that it is their mental illness that makes them homeless.

In this section a review of the opinions of some prominent psychiatrists regarding the homeless is offered. This review will focus on the following problems of the psychiatric view of homelessness: (1) the ecological fallacy, (2) methodological weakness, and (3) the limitations of psychiatric diagnosis.

The problems of the psychiatric view of homelessness are, of course, of much greater importance than intellectual and scientific concern. They have serious social policy complications regarding how best to resolve the homeless crisis. Most psychiatrists receive little training in social science and even less in research methodology. Perhaps because of the prestige bestowed on psychiatrists because of their medical degrees and their license to diagnose and prescribe treatments for "deviant" social behavior, they receive exaggerated deference for their opinions on social issues. For instance, their views on social issues are frequently featured and reported in the mass media. In an article entitled "Why Does Television Grovel at the Altar of Psychiatry?" and coauthored by the famous antipsychiatric psychiatrist Thomas S. Szasz, it is pointed out that:

> The willingness, perhaps even eagerness, on the part of the network reporters to be gulled by psychiatric explanations of human beings and their problems is astonishing—especially given their well-earned reputations for hard-

hitting investigative analyses in other areas of public concern in their efforts to satisfy the public's "right to know." (Vatz, Weinberg, & Szasz, 1985, p. D1).

It is, however, one thing for psychiatrists to be winners in the free market competition of opinions, and quite another when their interpretations influence and shape social policy. The effect of psychiatric explanations of homelessness on leading politicians is evident, for example, in the testimony before a Congressional hearing given by Los Angeles Mayor Tom Bradley. Bradley's city has been dubbed "Homeless Capital USA" by the media, and Bradley's testimony offered an explanation for his city's homeless population by describing his understanding of the composition of that population.

(1) The chronically disabled, suffering from alcoholism, drug abuse and/or mental illness, make up the largest subgroup. These individuals are found in high proportions on skid row and represent an estimated 55 percent of the homeless throughout the city.

(2) The second group consists of individuals who have experienced some kind of personal crisis. These homeless include runaways, young people who have been abused, or battered women. These people make up 29 percent of the city's homeless population.

(3) The third group, the economically disadvantaged, consists primarily of families and younger people who have lost their jobs and do not have local support systems. They constitute 16 percent of the homeless population in Los Angeles (Bradley, 1984).

THE ECOLOGICAL FALLACY

When two or more social conditions appear at the same time, it is tempting to assume they have some kind of connection. The ecological fallacy is committed when the occurrence of two or more large-scale but not necessarily connected social phenomena, such as homelessness and deinstitutionalization, is used to infer a connection between individuals and the causes of their behavior.

Despite the fact that most of the deinstitutionalized are sheltered in some way and that large epidemiological studies of the homeless (see Chapter 3) demonstrate that most of the homeless have never been in mental hospitals (Ohio, 1985; Farr, 1986), psychiatrists are responsible for perpetuating the belief that deinstitutionalization is the leading or primary cause of homelessness.

For example, Dr. R. Jones, in his review of this problem, states, "Foremost among the causes of homelessness is deinstitutionalization, a factor that demands the attention of the psychiatric profession" (Jones, 1983, p. 808). Others, like psychiatrist H. Richard Lamb, do not see deinstitutionalization, per se, as the cause of homelessness, but rather the way it was carried out.

> Is deinstitutionalization the cause of homelessness? Some would say yes and send the chronically mentally ill back to the hospitals. A main thesis of this chapter, however, is that problems such as homelessness are not the result of deinstitutionalization per se, but rather of the way deinstitutionalization has been implemented. Without deinstitutionalization it is unlikely there would be large numbers of homeless mentally ill (1984b, p. 55).

Until his most recent study, Dr. Rodger Farr, head of Adult Psychiatric Consultation Services, Los Angeles County Department of Mental Health, and member of the American Psychiatric Association's Task Force on the Homeless Mentally Ill, was one of the most outspoken proponents of the view that homelessness is the result of a plague of mental illness and deinstitutionalization and that most of the homeless are mentally ill. Farr wrote,

> What is of utmost importance is that 75% of the males and 90% of the females are suffering from chronic, incapacitating psychiatric illnesses. A large number of these people are overtly psychotic, and their behavior, at times, is so

bizarre that it would make them socially unacceptable and exclude them from most areas of any city. Many of the residents of skid row come from other states and communities. Our experience has shown that the vast majority have spent periods of time in mental institutions prior to coming to Los Angeles. It is not uncommon to find individuals who have been given money by their own communities for one-way tickets out of town. Frequently, they end up in Los Angeles. There is a high level of tolerance for deviant behavior in the skid row area, but even there, people may be excluded from local facilities if their behavior is too disruptive. The common bond among the majority of these people is that they are homeless, without families, and seem unable to meet many of the basic survival needs seen by many of us as inherited by living in this land of plenty (1982, pp. 2–3).

As discussed in Chapter 3, the deinstitutionalization of mental patients from state hospitals began in the 1950s. Gary J. Clarke, in a study of deinstitutionalization, contends that it has gone through three phases. In the first phase, between 1955 and 1964, there was a steady but slow decline of patients in mental hospitals, averaging about 8,300 per year nationally; in the second phase, between 1965 and 1975, the decline averaged 27,200 per year; and finally, in the present phase, "we are entering a third period marked by far slower rates of decline in inpatient populations" (1979, p. 463).

But where do former patients end up? Although some psychiatrists admit that "comprehensive data are lacking about the location of formerly hospitalized chronically mentally ill patients" (Bassuk & Lamb, 1986, p. 9), it is generally agreed that most are with their families, in nursing homes, in board and care homes, or in jails.

In the early years of deinstitutionalization, as many as two-thirds of the former patients stayed with their families and as many as one-third were in board and care homes (Lamb, 1984b, p. 63), while 6–10 percent of the population in state prisons may be the deinstitutionalized (Bassuk & Lamb, 1986, p. 19).

In a National Institute of Mental Health review of the data regarding the effects of deinstitutionalization, Dr. Howard H. Goldman concludes,

> Of an estimated 1.7 to 2.4 million chronic mentally ill Americans, approximately 150,000 have been residents of psychiatric hospitals for one year or longer, 750,000 reside in nursing homes, and 800,000 to 1,500,000 live at home or in a variety of community residences, including board-and-care homes (Goldman, Adams, & Taube, 1983, pp. 133–134).

Pamela Fischer and William Breakey, in a comprehensive review of the research literature regarding the relationship between deinstitutionalization and homelessness conclude,

> Though deinstitutionalization is often blamed for the recent increase in the absolute numbers of homeless people, empirical data to support this view are sparse. . . . Though the widespread dissatisfaction with its implementation in the United States in recent years may well be justified, there is a danger that the deinstitutionalization movement and shortcomings in community mental health services may become scapegoats for the various other forces in society that have contributed to the homelessness problem (1986, pp. 19–20).

Ironically, in 1986 Farr (with the assistance of two social scientists) was to conduct his own systematic research on the homeless mentally ill in Los Angeles, funded with $135,000 from the National Institute of Mental Health. The findings contradicted most of his earlier claims. Regarding deinstitutionalization, Farr concluded in his 1986 study,

> Only 14.8% of the sample as a whole, however, report having spent time in a state hospital. While these data do confirm a significant degree of past hospitalization among homeless individuals, then, they do not support the sim-

plistic notion that the homeless are largely comprised of ex-state hospital residents (Farr, Koegel, & Burnam, 1986, p. xiv).

Regarding his claims about how the deinstitutionalized get to Los Angeles, Farr finds in his 1986 study that his data "do *not* support the notion that Greyhound therapy occurs frequently enough to be affecting the overall number of homeless individuals in Los Angeles to any significant degree" (Farr, Koegel, & Burnam, 1986, p. 269).

It is undoubtedly true that some of the homeless are former mental patients, but as the epidemiological research clearly demonstrates, the majority of homeless individuals are not. The bulk of deinstitutionalization took place in the earlier decades of the 1950s, 1960s, and 1970s, but the dramatic increase in the national homeless population did not start until the late 1970s and continues through the 1980s. Perhaps psychiatrists were seduced into the deinstitutionalization argument by an uncritical acceptance of the Reagan administration claim that the economy was going through a recovery and thus that economic factors could not explain the increase in homelessness and by the fact that the many visible homeless are manifesting symptoms of the psychological distress of being homeless.

METHODOLOGICAL WEAKNESS

In addition to proposing that deinstitutionalization causes homelessness, some psychiatrists have maintained that most of the homeless are mentally ill and/or that their mental illness is the cause of the homelessness. These beliefs are largely the result of research studies with methodological weaknesses that have been conducted by psychiatrists and the mass media attention given to their flawed findings.

In 1983 the *New York Times* ran a story entitled "Studies Report Mental Illness in Most Homeless in 2 Cities" (Nelson, 1983), in which it was stated,

> The vast majority of homeless people studied in two urban areas are mentally ill and many have a history of psychiatric hospitalization, medical researchers have found.
>
> The authors of a study of 100 homeless who sought treatment at Bellevue Psychiatric Hospitals' emergency service in New York single out the policy of wholesale discharge of mental patients as playing a major role in the growing number of homeless on the streets of New York and other cities.

The authors of the Bellevue study included Dr. Steven Katz, a professor of clinical psychiatry at New York University, who became commissioner of the New York State Office of Mental Health in September 1983.

This study, which was published in *Hospital and Community Psychiatry* (Lipton, Sabatini, & Katz, 1983), is a remarkable case study of methodological naivete and the workings of "self-fulfilling prophesy" in research. The sample on which the sweeping claim that most of the homeless are mentally ill was based was not only non-random, but actually a group of only 90 psychiatric patients already admitted to Bellevue's psychiatric emergency service who happened to be homeless—of course they were diagnosed as having a "mental illness." As any first-year graduate student in the social sciences knows, you would need at least a random or systematically selected sample of homeless individuals to determine the incidence of mental illness among any homeless population, not a sample of the mentally ill who happen to be homeless!

The second study, conducted in Philadelphia (Arce et al., 1983), was based on a "retrospective review of the available records" of a non-probability sample of homeless individuals who were selected by an exclusionary screening process for admission to a temporary emergency shelter. While the Philadelphia group states, both in the abstract and in the text of the article, that its findings are based on a review of records, later in the text the findings are described as based on "psychiatric examination for 179 of the admissions." What the findings are actually based on is anyone's guess.

This study reported that 84.4 percent of the 179 residents

were diagnosed as having a mental illness. In direct contradiction to the *New York Times* description of the study, the authors conclude about their sample, "Contrary to popular belief, the group does not consist solely of former state hospital patients" (Arce et al., 1983, p. 816). In fact, it reported that only 35 percent had had some previous inpatient psychiatric treatment.

The study suffers from sample selection bias, in that the sample is a non-probability sample and only 193 out of 600 applicants for emergency shelter were admitted. In addition, the screening criteria are unspecified. The *ex post facto* psychiatric diagnosis of records is dubious; as the authors themselves point out, "the thoroughness of the records varied greatly" (p. 813).

In defense of these studies, it might be argued that they were exploratory in nature and produced early baseline information about the homeless, and that consequently, the numerous methodological flaws might be forgiven. But the social and ideological import given these studies by the mass media, which dramatized and exaggerated their claims, demands that the studies be given close scrutiny.

These two studies are not isolated cases. In a review of studies for the American Psychiatric Association Task Force Report on the Homeless Mentally Ill, concerned with the incidence of mental illness among the homeless, psychiatrists A. Anthony Arce and Michael J. Vergare (authors of the Philadelphia study) report about the methodological limits of the various studies. Nine studies that attempted to give psychiatric diagnoses were reviewed, but the reviewers warned, "Because the study settings and methodologies vary, the findings should be interpreted with caution" (Arce & Vergare, 1984, p. 80). Nevertheless, Dr. Lamb (quoted earlier in this chapter), chair of the American Psychiatric Association Task Force on the Homeless Mentally Ill and editor of the association's task force report, *The Homeless Mentally Ill* (1984), and Dr. John A. Talbott, the association's president, based the recommendations of the task force at least partially on the findings of these studies. The Arce and Vergare review is included in the book under the title "Identifying and Characterizing the Mentally Ill among the Homeless" and serves as the pivotal epidemiological chapter. In reference to the studies reviewed by Arce and Vergare, Lamb and Talbott state,

> The most methodologically sound studies performed thus far indicate that among the total population of homeless persons, there is a prevalence of about 40% with major mental illness (this is, schizophrenia and major affective disorder) (Lamb & Talbott, 1986, pp. 498).

It is worth the effort to briefly examine the review of these studies, because they are the basis of the claim that chronic mental illness is pervasive among the homeless. Arce and Vergare, in the widely quoted conclusion of their review, stated, "It is evident that in most universes of homeless people, between 25 percent and 50 percent have serious and chronic forms of mental illness" (1984, p. 88).

The first study they reviewed was conducted in England in 1955. (What can it tell us about the homeless in the United States during the 1980s?) It consisted of a non-random sample of 100 males admitted to a psychiatric unit. The method of diagnosis is not reviewed.

The second study was also conducted in the 1950s and was a review of 101 cases of homeless men. "The methods used to gather data are unspecified," (p. 81) as well as the method of diagnosis.

The third, a 1970 study, was a review of case summaries of admissions to the Manhattan Bowery Project, a treatment program for alcoholics, and reported on 200 non-random selected admissions. "The author did not detail the exact procedures used to reach these diagnoses" (Arce & Vergare, 1984, p. 81).

A fourth study conducted in 1971 interviewed 122 men in hostels. No review of methods is done by Arce and Vergare.

For the fifth, a 1976 comparative study of 85 subjects from Edinburgh and 50 subjects from Chicago, Arce and Vergare give no review of methods, sampling strategy, or operationalization and standardization of diagnostic protocol.

The sixth study reviewed was the highly flawed Lipton, Sabatini, and Katz 1983 Bellevue study discussed above.

The seventh study, conducted by Harvard psychiatrist Ellen Bassuk, which was indicated to be "in press," consisted of interviews with 78 homeless men, women, and children in a Boston shelter. No exposition of methods was given in the review. When the study was actually published (Bassuk, Rubin, & Lauriot, 1986), it turned out that the sample was not representative of shelter users and was non-random.

The eighth study reviewed was the ex post facto review of 193 records (Arce et al., 1983) discussed earlier in this chapter.

The ninth and final study considered was a 1983 "follow-up" study by Vergare and Arce of admissions to a shelter. No discussion of methodology is offered in the review.

This review of research studies has probably contributed much to perpetuating the myth that most of the homeless are mentally ill. Much to do, in other words, has been made on the basis of very little and extremely flawed research.

The review quoted earlier by Fischer and Breakey (1986) is a more rigorous treatment of studies of mental disorders among the homeless than Arce and Vergare's. Four recent studies, including the Lipton, Arce, and Bassuk studies outlined above, were evaluated. Fischer and Breakey concluded, "Each of these drew a restricted sample from a single service site or from a single type of service site; thus, none in itself gives a broad view of the homeless population" (1986, p. 15).

THE LIMITATIONS OF PSYCHIATRIC DIAGNOSIS

Various research studies raise serious questions regarding the reliability and validity of psychiatric diagnosis; psychiatric diagnoses of homeless individuals may be even more problematic. In a report in the *New York Times* Science Times section (Goleman, 1985), it was revealed that

> Some psychiatrists believe severe harm has been done as a result of misdiagnoses. Mistaking various forms of depression for schizophrenia is the most frequent error, according to the report, and the harm is said to be caused essentially by the use of powerful but inappropriate drugs (p. 19).

The research on misdiagnoses referred to in the *New York Times* story was conducted by doctors Alan Lipton and Franklin Simon at the Manhattan Psychiatric Center. The research found that as many as 75 percent of the patients had been misdiagnosed, and the researchers believed that this rate of misdiagnosis is probably "about average" for state mental hospitals. The misdiagnoses primarily involved mistaking affective disorders for schizophrenia. Out of a random sample of 131 patients, 89 originally had been diagnosed as schizophrenic, but on reevaluation the schizophrenia diagnoses held up in only 16 cases (1985, pp. 368–372).

The rate of misdiagnosis may be even higher for blacks. Dr. William B. Lawson found that "Recent research suggests that Blacks and other minorities are at a greater risk than whites of being misdiagnosed" (1986, p. B2; see also Ziegler, 1986). Psychiatrist B. Jones, director of psychiatry at Lincoln Medical and Mental Health Center, Bronx, NY, stressed that cultural differences in expression of emotion and behavior may result in misdiagnosis of Blacks because psychiatric diagnosis rests "almost entirely" on observation of behavior (Jones & Gray 1986).

None of the existing psychiatric literature on the incidence of mental illness among the homeless reports diagnoses relative to the race of the subjects. The national data sets on the demographics of the contemporary homeless (see Chapter 1) demonstrate that nonwhites constitute at least half of most homeless populations or that nonwhites are disproportionately represented among various homeless populations. Given these facts, at least suspicion is demanded regarding the diagnosis of mental illness among homeless populations. If 75 percent of the patients in a highly controlled setting like a state mental hospital can be misdiagnosed, how much more likely is it that individuals on the street or in a shelter have been misdiagnosed. Even more problematic is the diagnosis of homeless individuals based on retrospective reviews of their records.

There are five studies, often cited, that attempt to give psychiatric diagnostic prevalence or incidence rates for homeless samples. The findings of these studies vary greatly regarding incidence of leading psychiatric disorders (schizophrenia, personality disorders, and affective disorders). Limitations of sampling strategies, representativeness of samples, different diagnostic techniques, and the small size of most samples also plague these studies. (See Table 4.3.)

The Lipton, Sabatini, and Katz study (1983) reports the highest rate of chronic mental illness (72.7 percent schizophrenia), but as discussed previously this study is so seriously flawed that its findings and conclusions are unreliable. In the Arce et al. study (1983), lower rates of mental illness are reported than in the Lipton study, but it, too, suffers from the serious methodological limitations indicated earlier.

A stronger epidemiological study of mental illness among a homeless sample is provided by the Fischer and Breakey study (1986), which actually was part of a larger National Institute of Mental Health Epidemiological Catchment Area survey of mental illness in eastern Baltimore, which randomly sampled 1,387 "households." Out of that sample was derived a subsample of 51 homeless individuals. The diagnoses, however, were not made by psychiatrists, although the Diagnostic Interview Schedule (DIS) was administered by trained lay interviewers. The DIS is a survey questionnaire by which it is contended that psychiatric diagnoses can be derived through a "computerized algorithm."

The incidence rates for schizophrenia and affective disorders of the Fischer study are strikingly lower than those of the Lipton and Arce studies. While this study is methodologically stronger, the strength of its conclusions is limited by the extremely small size of its homeless sample.

In the Bassuk study (1986a), 80 mothers non-randomly selected and interviewed in an unrepresentative sample of family shelters in Boston were diagnosed by an unknown number of psychiatrists and one psychologist. The rate of schizophrenia was low (3 percent); however, a high rate (71 percent) of various forms of personality disorders was found.

Finally, in what is the most methodologically rigorous study of mental illness among a homeless population, the Farr, Koegel, and Burnam study (1986) (ironically the same Farr responsible for many of the exaggerated and unsupported statements about the homeless discussed earlier) found that 28

TABLE 4.3

Reported Rates of Selected Mental Illnesses among the Homeless

Researchers	Sample Size	Sampling Strategy	Diagnostic Technique	Selected Diagnostic Categories (%)		
				Schizophrenia	*Personality Disorder*	*Affective Disorder*
Lipton, Sabatini, & Katz	90	Non-random	ex post facto review of records	72.2	12.2	6.7
Arce et al.	179	Non-random	ex post facto review of records	37.4	6.7	5.6
Fischer et al.	51	Random	diagnostic interview schedule	2.0*	11.8*	2.0*
Bassuk	80	Non-random	psychiatric interview	3.0	71.0	10.0
Farr, Koegel, & Burnam	379	Random	diagnostic interview schedule	11.5*	17.4*	19.9*

*Within six months.

Studies Evaluated: A. Lipton, A. Sabatini, & S. Katz, Down and out in the city: The homeless mentally ill, *Hospital and Community Psychiatry*, 36(9), 817–821; A. Arce et al., A psychiatric profile of street people admitted to an emergency shelter, *Hospital and Community Psychiatry*, 34(9), 812–817; P. Fischer et al., mental health and social characteristics of the homeless: A survey of mission users, *American Journal of Public Health*, 76(5), 519–523; E. Bassuk (Ed.), *The mental health needs of homeless persons* (San Francisco: Jossey-Bass, 1986); R. Farr, P. Koegel, & A. Burnam, *A study of homelessness and mental illness in the skid row area of Los Angeles* (Los Angeles: Los Angeles County Department of Mental Health, 1986).

percent of its sample "as a whole meet our criteria for severe and chronic mental illness" (p. 141). Specifically, 11.5 percent were schizophrenic, 17.4 percent had personality disorders, and 19.9 percent had affective disorders (the categories were not mutually exclusive; thus an individual might be counted more than once).

The Farr study is good in terms of its sampling strategy and sample size, and the psychiatric diagnoses were made with the DIS.

All of these studies report that the incidence of various mental illnesses is significantly higher than in the general population. This is certainly true, but probably not as true if the incidence rates are controlled by social class. Sociologically, the homeless are obviously at the very bottom of the social stratification system, however operationalized. The homeless can be classified as members of the lower working class, as the lower lower class, or as members of the bottom of the "underclass." Classic epidemiological studies of the incidence of mental illness among social classes have established the differential rates of psychiatric morbidity between social classes.

The 1958 classic *Social Class and Mental Illness*, by A. B. Hollingshead and F. C. Redlich, found an inverse relationship between social class and being a mental patient. The prevalence rate per 100,000 for Class I and II (the highest social classes) was 553, while for the lowest, Class V, the rate was 1,668. Hollingshead and Redlich also discovered that the type of diagnosis of mental illness varied with the social class status of the patient. About 35 percent of the upper- and middle-class patients, but 90 percent of the lower-class patients, were labelled psychotic (p. 10).

A similar conclusion was drawn in one of the most extensive studies ever made of mental illness in New York City, by L. Srole (Srole, Langer, & Michael, 1962) which found that 12.5 percent of those in the highest six socioeconomic status (SES) groups had a psychological impairment, compared to 47.3 percent of those in the lowest SES groups.

In a review of 44 mental health prevalence studies, B. P. Dohrenwend and B. S. Dohrenwend (1969) found "The most consistent result in an inverse relationship between social class and reported rates of psychological disorder" (p. 165).

None of the studies of mental illness among the homeless attempt to control for social class or race in interpreting the implications of their findings among the homeless. Even if these findings are taken at face value, a consideration of social class would put them in a different light. Aside from this consideration, however, is the issue of the reliability and validity of diagnostic techniques and criteria in assessing "mental illness" among the homeless.

LIMITATIONS OF DIAGNOSTIC CRITERIA WHEN APPLIED TO THE HOMELESS

Among homeless samples in which an attempt has been made to give subjects some type of psychiatric diagnosis, the diagnostic labels of personality disorder, schizophrenia, and affective disorders are the ones most often given. In reviewing the diagnostic criteria of these disorders and their variants as described in the American Psychiatric Association's *Diagnostic and Statistical Manual of Mental Disorders* (DSM, 1980), it becomes evident that in some cases it may be difficult to distinguish chronic psychiatric symptoms from the effects and demands of being homeless. Three specific examples follow.

Consider the diagnostic criteria for antisocial personality disorder, which include

> Inability to sustain consistent work behavior as indicated by too frequent job changes or significant unemployment (e.g., six months or more in five years when expected to work), . . .
>
> Failure to accept social norms with respect to lawful behavior, . . .
>
> Irritability and aggressiveness, . . .
>
> Failure to honor financial obligations, . . .
>
> Disregard for the truth, . . .
>
> Recklessness (DSM, 1980, p. 320).

These are only examples of the criteria for antisocial personality disorder. An individual meeting at least four of these criteria, many of which may well be culturally and class biased, may be diagnosed as having this disorder.

Psychiatrist Farr and his associates also acknowledged this problem in their study (Farr, Koegel, & Burnam, 1986). In fact, they had to eliminate several items from the DIS to control for the consequences of homelessness, which mimic symptoms of antisocial personality disorder. Theoretical justification for the elimination of items was given as follows:

> Complications specific to the use of this diagnosis with a homeless problem are even more apparent. Many individuals, for instance, become homeless when they lose a job and are unable to find a new one. Finding themselves homeless, their energies become focused on survival—on finding a place to sleep and getting food into their stomachs. These tasks often become full-time endeavors in and of themselves; they have no time to do anything other than seek those things, and may become less equipped to present themselves in a marketable light. Day labor jobs sometimes become their only source of employment. Living in Skid Row where they have the greatest chance of finding facilities which can meet their basic subsistence needs, they find themselves in danger: danger from the authorities, who might arrest them for as minor an infraction as jaywalking and put them in jail when they cannot afford to pay the fine; and danger from those who would victimize them for whatever little they have. To protect themselves, they may begin carrying weapons. All of these things—not having a regular place to live for a month or more, not working for long periods of time, having many jobs in a short period of time, having had frequent arrests, carrying a weapon—are symptoms which count toward a diagnosis of antisocial personality (though it should be stressed that a history of antisocial behavior throughout one's childhood must be present as well for a diagnosis to be made). As such, homeless individuals are at risk of being labeled antisocial precisely because they are homeless and because of the consequences of being homeless (pp. 133–134).

The second example concerns what is called "affective disorders," particularly "major depressive episodes." In general, affective disorders involve a disturbance of mood. "Mood refers to a prolonged emotion that colors the whole psychic life; it generally involves either depression or elation" (DSM 1980, p. 205).

Select criteria for the diagnoses of major depressive episodes include poor appetite, weight loss, insomnia, psychomotor agitation, "loss of interest or pleasure in usual activities," fatigue, feelings of worthlessness, diminished ability to think, and suicidal ideation (DSM 1980, pp. 213–214). Four or more of these symptoms must be present nearly every day for two weeks.

It is unlikely that there is a homeless person anywhere who hasn't experienced at least four of these symptoms. As the empirical findings of Chapter 1 revealed, 70 percent of the Los Angeles sample reported being depressed and the mean duration of depression for the sample was eleven weeks! The leading reasons for being depressed were no job, no money, and separation from family. It certainly is conceivable that the "mood disorders" of homeless persons are the result of their situation and not of a chronic illness. Like some other psychiatrists, Bassuk, when interviewed for a popular magazine, responded to the question, "Do people become mentally ill as a result of being homeless?" by answering, "It's my impression that very few do. In our two studies, we found that mental disorders began before a person became homeless. However, if anyone has been traumatized by homelessness, obviously it can leave lasting scars" (Bassuk, 1986b, p. 88).

Some psychiatrists even go so far as to imply that since some mental illnesses are genetically caused and most of the homeless are mentally ill, homelessness may be biologically determined! Dr. David Tomb, professor of psychiatry at the University of Utah Medical School and medical director of the Western Institute of Neuropsychiatry, had his views described in the following way: "Tomb said the major mental illness that causes people to wander the streets is schizophrenia, which he said is a biological inherited condition" (Palmer, 1986).

Actually, as presented earlier, in most of the studies conducted by psychiatrists (except for the Lipton study, from which generalizations cannot be made) the majority of homeless persons studied were not, by any method, diagnosed as schizophrenic. Nevertheless, the issue of the origin and validity of the diagnostic criteria for schizophrenia has a long history of controversy within the psychiatric community and especially between that community and social scientists and psychologists.

DSM (1980) points out that "schizophrenia always involves deterioration from a previous level of functioning during some phase of the illness in such areas as work, social relations and self-care" (p. 181). Diagnostic criteria also include "characteristic symptoms involving multiple psychological processes." These processes may include such disturbances as delusions, incoherence, hallucinations, inappropriateness of emotion, lack of self-direction and goal-directed behavior, withdrawal of involvement, and various psychomotor disturbances (pp. 182–184).

It is not contended here that no schizophrenia exists among the homeless. But given the limitations in reliability and validity of psychiatric diagnoses and the circumstances under which studies attempting to detect mental illness among the homeless have been carried out, it is probable that some homeless persons displaying the above symptoms may have in fact been misdiagnosed.

The DSM, however, does caution that the diagnosis of schizophrenia "is made more commonly among the lower socioeconomic groups. The reasons for this are unclear, but may involve downward social drift, lack of upward socioeconomic mobility, and high stress" (p. 186). Regarding the role of genetic factors in the etiology of schizophrenic disorders, the DSM also points out, "Although genetic factors have been proven to be involved in the development of the illness, the existence of a substantial discordance rate, even in monozygotic twins, indicates the importance of nongenetic factors" (p. 186).

Dr. Richard Warner, in his epidemiological research (1985) on the incidence of schizophrenia and its relation to fluctuations in the economy, found that, "the production of mental illness increases with each setback in the economy and with the reduction in the call for labor" (p. 56). Based on a review of 87 research studies on recovery rates for schizophrenia, he concludes that "the state of the economy appears to be linked to outcome in schizophrenia" (p. 70). At the time of the Great Depression in the 1930s, Warner found, for example, that the rate of recovery dropped to half (12 percent) of what it had been before the Depression.

Warner's research suggests that even among those individuals with a propensity to develop schizophrenic symptoms, the manifestation, duration, and remission of symptoms is highly correlated with economic fluctuations. He also suggests that the inability of psychiatry to comprehend the political economy of schizophrenia leads to a reductionist interpretation that focuses on hereditary factors. When the economy is weak and rates of schizophrenia are high, Warner believes many psychiatrists, not prepared to critique socioeconomic structures, turn out of pessimism to explanations of mental illness that emphasize biological factors (pp. 137–138).

Dr. Lamb (quoted earlier) goes as far as to contend that in many cases homelessness itself is a symptom of mental illness.

> Too much emphasis on shelters can only delay our coming to grips with the underlying problems that result in homelessness. . . . Most mental health professionals are disinclined to treat "street people" or "transients." Moreover, in the case of many of the homeless, we are working with persons whose lack of trust and desire for autonomy cause them to not give us their real names, to refuse our services, and to move along because of their fear of closeness, of losing their autonomy, or of acquiring a mentally ill identity (1984b, pp. 58–59).

Elsewhere, Lamb and Talbott (1986) write that "the overall conclusion of the (APA) Task Force was that homelessness among the mentally ill is essentially a symptom of the basic underlying problems facing the chronically mentally ill generally in this country" (p. 500).

In a blatant blaming-the-victim argument, which is reminiscent of that pre-Civil War psychiatric diagnosis called "drapetomania," an affliction that "caused" black slaves to run away from their masters, Lamb offers the affliction he calls "the tendency to Drift." Apparently this "symptom" of mental illness has reached epidemic proportions in the 1980s at precisely the same time as the emergence of the hundreds of thousands who constitute the new urban homeless. They drift, according to Lamb, because

> apart from their desire to outrun their problems, their symptoms, and their failures, many have great difficulty achieving closeness and intimacy. A fantasy of finding closeness elsewhere encourages them to move on. Yet all too often, if they do stumble into an intimate relationship or find themselves in a residence where there is caring and closeness and sharing, the increased anxiety they experience creates a need to run.
>
> They drift also in search of autonomy, as a way of denying their dependency, and out of a desire for an isolated life-style. Lack of money often makes them unwelcome, and they may be evicted by family and friends. And they drift because of a reluctance to become involved in a mental health treatment program or a supportive out-of-home environment, such as a halfway house or board-and-care home, that would give them a mental patient identity and make them part of the mental health system: they do not want to see themselves as ill (1984b, pp. 64–65).

Others become homeless because they "are not proficient at coping with the stresses of the world"; "they are vulnerable to eviction"; or they have "an inability to deal with difficult or even ordinary landlord-tenant situations" (Lamb & Talbott 1986, p. 499).

Evidence presented earlier indicated that the majority of the deinstitutionalized and the chronically mentally ill are in fact not homeless. It is illogical to contend that mental illness of any kind, per se, causes someone to become homeless. If Lamb were to discuss specifically how the problems of the job and housing markets, the lack of community mental health centers, rising poverty rates, and political decisions that restrict and cut back on social welfare programs interact with the vulnerability of mental illness to force an individual down the path of homelessness, his theories would be more creditable.

In a 1986 Los Angeles Legal Aid suit against the County of Los Angeles (Rensch 1986), it was argued that county requirements and procedures for obtaining General Relief (GR) were discriminatory towards the homeless mentally ill. Evidence was presented demonstrating that GR applicants with a mental disability were often not successful in negotiating the bureaucratic maze to obtain welfare. Dr. Lamb served as an "expert" witness on behalf of the defendant, the Los Angeles County Department of Public Social Services.

Lamb's testimony is a fascinating instance in which a blaming-the-victim theory is put to practical use. Lamb argued that the welfare department was not at fault for its inadequate handling of the homeless mentally ill. Instead, he placed the blame directly on the homeless. Lamb testified,

> Chronically mentally ill persons do not like to admit their inadequacies and tend to deny their inadequacies and instead blame the situation. In working with chronically mentally ill persons, one finds this again and again. It is a way of maintaining some semblance of their self-esteem to blame an agency such as DPSS or the courts or a hospital, rather than to acknowledge that they are inadequate and mentally ill. This may be a necessary psychological defense for many mentally ill persons. However, it is also important that we recognize this as a defense and not necessarily as reality (Rensch, 1986).

In all of the published psychiatric literature regarding mental illness among the homeless, there are no comprehensive analyses of the relationship between diagnostic symptoms and the identification, degree, and severity of psychosocial stressors. As previously indicated, unemployment is a severe psychosocial stressor that can result in various signs of distress, including symptoms that mimic schizophrenia. Evidence, as well as common sense, indicates that the condition of homelessness contributes significantly to physical and psychological morbidity. Perhaps in their rush to judgment, psychiatrists are not diligently controlling for the consequences of homelessness, which may mimic chronic mental disorders, from bona fide symptoms of mental illness.

Dr. William Clem, an expert on hypothermia at the Santa Monica Hospital Medical Center, studied the rates of hypothermia reported at Los Angeles County–USC Medical Center and those reported at Bellevue Hospital in New York. Dr. Clem found that more cases of hypothermia among the homeless are reported in Los Angeles than in New York City (Clem, 1984). Hypothermia, which is defined as a core body temperature below 90–95 degrees Fahrenheit and has a mortality rate of 50 percent, can occur as a result of exposure to temperatures as high as 50 degrees Fahrenheit, depending on other factors such as exposure to dampness and the age and nutritional conditions of the individual. Of the hypothermia patients seen at LA-USC Medical Center, 80 to 90 percent were homeless. In addition to the risk of death to these homeless patients from hypothermia, Dr. Gary Rapaport a specialist in emergency medicine at California Hospital who treats approximately 1,500 homeless patients per year, has found that

> based on my research, training and experience, I can say that homeless patients suffer from a variety of medical conditions and diseases in a higher incidence than patients in a normal population who have shelter. In particular, homeless patients suffer hypothermia from accidental exposure, have medical consequences which range from severe brain damage, renal failure, pneumonia, cardiac arrest and ultimately death. The fact is that hypothermia severely affects all of the organ systems which can lead to conditions causing death (Ross, 1984).

A nurse practitioner, Rosemary Occheogrosso of the Hospitality Free Clinic in the Los Angeles skid row, which serves about 130 homeless clients per week, relates her experiences with the homeless in the following way:

> Medical problems to which homeless people are especially susceptible include hypothermia, hyperthermia, skin infec-

tions, pediculosis, respiratory disorders (including pneu-
monia and tuberculosis), dependent edema, stasis ulcers,
tetanus, stress (including, e.g., depression psychosis),
trauma associated with assault, and alcoholism. . . .

I don't know if people come to the streets crazy or if
they are driven crazy by life on the streets. But I am sure
of one thing. People on the edge are pushed over. . . .

Skid Row is the most dangerous neighborhood in the
city. I must see an assault victim every week. I've seen
large lacerations, broken bones, the gamut. And we don't
see the worst cases. They go straight to County/U.S.C.
Hospital. Or to the morgue (Ross, 1984).

The risks associated with being homeless include not only
health and psychological risks, but also the risk of being a
victim of crime. The survey of homeless people in Los Angeles
reported in Chapter 1 found that 34 percent reported that
they had been victims of a crime in the previous six months.
According to Dr. Rapaport,

Many of the homeless I treat are victims of gunshot
wounds, knife wounds and trauma associated with second-
ary contusions from baseball bats, tire irons or bottles. The
homeless patients lack security and are the walking prey of
wandering street gangs. Sometimes homeless patients will
tell me their crutches have been stolen and I have observed homeless blind people who have been beaten and
robbed (Ross, 1984).

All of these conditions must obviously be recognized as
"psychosocial stressors" that logically would contribute to the
mental state of homeless individuals. Can there be any doubt
that any "average normal" person exposed to the health and
crime risks of homelessness would face serious problems in
"adaptive functioning"? Yet some psychiatrists continue to
argue that it is primarily the attributes of some of the homeless
themselves that essentially explain their condition (Farr, 1982;
Bassuk, 1986a; Lamb & Talbott, 1986).

Clinical psychologist Kevin Flynn, who has worked with

the homeless in the Los Angeles skid row for several years, summarized his experience of the effect of homelessness on mental health in his testimony in two lawsuits, as follows:

> My experience, the extant literature, and common sense all indicate that homeless persons experience severe, and frequently overwhelming, stress which leads to clinically recognizable emotional and psychological problems (Blair, 1985)

> I have noted that individuals without shelter, particularly during the cold . . . season, suffer from high levels of anxiety, depression, withdrawal, tearfulness, hopelessness, disorientation, reduced levels of cognitive functioning, hyperalertness, sleep disturbance, exhaustion and psychophysiological disorders.
>
> In general the lack of proper, reasonably safe shelter contributes to the psychological deterioration of relatively normal individuals and exacerbates the mental disorders in those individuals with a history of psychiatric disturbance (Ross, 1984).

There can be no doubt that most of the homeless suffer from the psychological effects of unemployment and the lack of a home. By and large, the mental health needs of the homeless, like their basic need for shelter, food, and health care, go unmet. A minority of the homeless have been psychiatric patients at one time or another, and some suffer from chronic mental illness. Nevertheless, the attempt by some "advocacy" psychiatrists to convince the public and social policymakers that homelessness is primarily a mental health issue, is perhaps an unwitting ideological use of a blaming-the-victim perspective. This is true even for those who, while not contending that all of the homeless are mentally ill, nonetheless move the focus from homelessness as a societal problem to the characteristics and attributes of the victims of unemployment and homelessness.

By exposing the inadequacy and even inaccuracy of the psychiatric perspective on homelessness, no attempt is made here to neglect the importance of meeting the mental health needs of those without homes. Adequate funding for community mental programs, for outreach programs, and for case management must be an essential part of any long-term strategy to resolve the homelessness crisis. Exaggerated or misleading claims about the epidemiology of chronic illness among the homeless will not help; instead, they tend to shift society's attention away from the primary causes and consequences of homelessness.

SUMMARY

Unambiguous epidemiological evidence exists indicating that the majority of the homeless are not deinstitutionalized from mental hospitals. Also, the majority of the homeless would not require psychiatric hospitalization.

There is no definitive evidence to support the claim that most or even a substantial minority of the homeless suffer from chronic mental illnesses, either predating their homelessness or not.

Evidence, however, does exist that most of the homeless suffer from the psychological stress and demoralization that results from economic and housing displacement and psychological and social disaffiliation.

Public acceptance of the constant portrayal by the mass media of the homeless as mentally ill may serve the ideological function of obscuring the growing socioeconomic inequality in the United States.

Chapter 5

JOB AND HOUSING DISPLACEMENT

The Contemporary Path to Mass Disaffiliation

In a 1925 book entitled *Social Pathology*, sociologists Stuart Queen and Delbert Mann wrote about the relationship of hard economic times and "homeless men."

> Unattached men are demanded to build bridges, tunnels, railroads and irrigation systems, to cut timber and harvest the crops. They go here and there to rough, uncomfortable parts of the country, breaking the way for others after the fashion of pioneers. They also constitute a part of our "labor reserve." It is they who are first discharged when business is slack and the last to be re-employed. . . . In a very real sense they are the product of a badly organized economic system (p. 203).

Queen and Mann realized that homelessness was not simply the product of economic factors. They also suggested that a certain type of personality defect, *Wanderlust*, "a strong spirit of restlessness," interacted with a troubled economy to produce homeless men. An example they gave is young men who were anxious to go west to fight Indians and become cowboys (p. 204). The parallel between Wanderlust and psychiatrist H. Richard Lamb's "theory" of *drift* (discussed in the preceding chapter) is tempting!

But, as psychiatrist Richard Warner reminds us, "Whichever part of the picture we study, nevertheless it seems likely that the labor market is closely involved in the social production and perpetuation of psychosis" (1985, p. 135).

The concept of a "labor reserve" or "industrial reserve army," however, gets right to the core as an important contributing theoretical explanation of the job displacement that often precipitates housing displacement.

The evidence regarding the relatively high rates of unemployment and underemployment and the process of deindustrialization described in Chapter 3 suggest that the concept of the industrial reserve army may again be a timely explanation for some of our leading social problems. In fact, some significant contemporary studies of social problems find the concept useful (Anderson, 1974; Piven & Cloward, 1982; Szymanski, 1983; Warner, 1985).

In *Capital*, Karl Marx viewed economic insecurity, particularly unemployment, as one of the inherent structural products of a capitalistic mode of production. He used the concepts of *surplus population* and *industrial reserve army* to refer to that part of the working class that is unemployed (1965, p. 628). The concepts of surplus population and industrial reserve army were central to Marx's analysis of what he believed were the contradictions of a capitalist society; these concepts played an important role in what Marx considered to be one of the "absolute laws" of capitalistic development.

For Marx, the accumulation of capital progresses with a constant qualitative change in its composition. With the increasing rationalization of production—as with automation—and thus the production by each individual worker of relatively more wealth, there is consequently an increase in constant capital—land, machinery, factories, and so on—and a decrease in the need for variable capital—human labor power (p. 629). It is this structural decrease in the need for variable capital that results in an increasing surplus population and industrial reserve army, that is, in the number of unemployed and the people they support. As Marx put it,

> it is capitalistic accumulation itself that constantly pro-
> duces, and produces in the direct ratio of its own energy
> and extent, a relatively redundant population of labour-
> ers, i.e., a population of greater extent than suffices for
> the average needs of the self-expansion of capital, and
> therefore a surplus-population (p. 630).

While the unemployed are a consequence of structural features of capitalistic developments, the unemployed also fulfill certain "functions" for a capitalistic society.

1. Unemployment creates a mass of workers that can readily
    be exploited for the sudden development of new indus-
    tries, without detracting from the general level of produc-
    tion in established areas.
2. Unemployment enriches the capitalist class by enabling
    that class to employ fewer workers at lower wages, thus
    increasing profits. Additionally, those who are employed
    are better regulated and controlled and can thus be made
    to be more productive. This is possible when employed
    workers know that at any time they could easily be replaced
    by an unemployed worker who is anxious to make a living.
    Marx stated,

> The condemnation of one part of the working class to
> enforced idleness by the over-work of the other part, and
> the converse, becomes a means of enriching the individual
> capitalists, and accelerates at the same time the production
> of the industrial reserve army on a scale corresponding
> with the advance of social accumulation (p. 636).

3. The division of the working class into employed and
    unemployed may inhibit the struggle of the working class
    to acquire a larger share of the social wealth produced.
    The old strategy of "divide and conquer" is often evi-

denced when employed workers are so threatened by losing their jobs that they turn against their fellow workers who are unemployed instead of against the economic system that structurally produces their economic insecurity. Competition for the jobs that do exist may thus mitigate against the solidarity of the working class and the development of working class consciousness. As Marx put it,

> The industrial reserve army, during the periods of stagnation and average prosperity, weighs down the active labour-army; during the periods of over-production and paroxysm, it holds its pretensions in check. Relative surplus population is therefore the pivot upon which the law of demand and supply of labour works. It confines the field of action of this law within the limits absolutely convenient to the activity of exploitation and to the domination of capital (p. 639).

4. Finally, Marx contended that the "absolute law of capital accumulation" results in the increased relative economic, social, and psychological misery of sections of the working class. Of particular interest in the following statement by Marx is the connection he makes between alienation and unemployment:

> The law, finally that always equilibrates the relative surplus-population, or industrial reserve army, to the extent and energy of accumulation, this law rivets the labourer to capital more firmly than the wedges of Vulcan did Prometheus to the rock. It establishes an accumulation of misery, agony of toil, slavery, ignorance, brutality, mental degradation, at the opposite pole, i.e., on the side of the class that produces its own product in the form of capital (p. 644).

Thus Marx contended that as capital accumulates so does the alienation and misery of the employed and unemployed members of the working class.

Over 143 years ago Friedrich Engels, Marx's close collaborator, described the condition of members of an industrial reserve army who became homeless.

> In London fifty thousand human beings get up every morning, not knowing where they are to lay their heads at night. . . . They sleep where they find a place, in passages, arcades, in corners where the police and the owners leave them undisturbed. A few individuals find their way to the refuges which are managed, here and there, by private charity, others sleep on the benches in the parks (1973, p. 71).

It is disturbing that this description written so long ago could apply to almost any major U.S. city today!

Whether or not we agree with Marx's "absolute law of capital accumulation" or any other aspect of his theories regarding the role of unemployment, evidence presented earlier about deindustrialization, the rate of unemployment, and the physical, psychological, and social consequences of unemployment indicate that structural trends in the contemporary U.S. economy are resulting in massive economic dislocations and displacement of millions of individuals.

Economic displacement, in combination with housing displacement, as outlined previously, are the social structural roots of the current homeless crisis.

The link between unemployment/underemployment and homelessness is clear both at the macro- and micro-levels of analysis. As American industry "disinvests," unemployment rates go up. When this occurs at more or less the same time as a decrease in the low-income housing market, increases in the incidence of homelessness result.

Reasons why a disaffiliated homeless person may gravitate to skid row areas were suggested by Bogue in 1963. (See Figure 5.1.) There are two basic themes in Bogue's list of reasons, one economic, the other social. The skid row areas provide relatively cheap lodgings and other services: there are shelters, "free" clinics, and access to temporary employment markets. For example, in Los Angeles an eligible homeless person may receive a county welfare housing voucher for temporary

FIGURE 5.1

Theoretical Model: From Social Disaffiliation/Displacement to "Skid Row" Way of Life

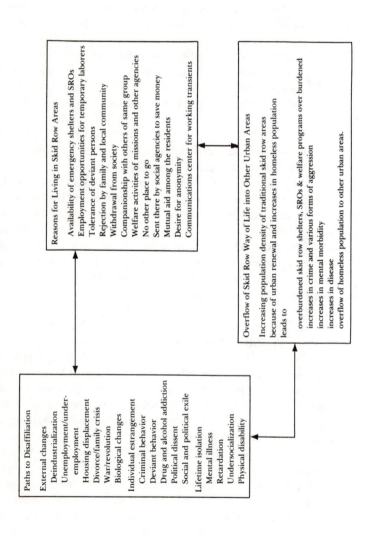

Paths to Disaffiliation

External changes
  Deindustrialization
  Unemployment/under-
    employment
  Housing displacement
  Divorce/family crisis
  War/revolution
  Biological changes
Individual estrangement
  Criminal behavior
  Deviant behavior
  Drug and alcohol addiction
  Political dissent
  Social and political exile
Lifetime isolation
  Mental illness
  Retardation
  Undersocialization
  Physical disability

Reasons for Living in Skid Row Areas

Availability of emergency shelters and SROs
Employment opportunities for temporary laborers
Tolerance of deviant persons
Rejection by family and local community
Withdrawal from society
Companionship with others of same group
Welfare activities of missions and other agencies
No other place to go
Sent there by social agencies to save money
Mutual aid among the residents
Desire for anonymity
Communications center for working transients

Overflow of Skid Row Way of Life into Other Urban Areas

Increasing population density of traditional skid row areas
because of urban renewal and increases in homeless population
leads to

  overburdened skid row shelters, SROs & welfare programs over burdened
  increases in crime and various forms of aggression
  increases in mental morbidity
  increases in disease
  overflow of homeless population to other urban areas.

emergency shelter, but virtually all the hotel/motel voucher vendors are located in skid row (Robertson, Ropers, & Boyer, 1984). The system thus forces homeless people to live in skid row if they want to use this form of assistance.

Given the largest increase in the homeless population since the economic depression of the 1930s, today's homeless population density overburdens the limited resources of skid row. In a study of emergency shelter and welfare lodging in Los Angeles, researchers found that only 9 percent of the Los Angeles County estimated homeless population of 33,800 (which excludes the estimated 15,000 in SROs) are accommodated on any given night by a combination of private emergency shelter, county emergency lodging vouchers, and emergency lodging checks (Robertson, Ropers, & Boyer, 1984).

Not only are the traditional skid row agencies unable to provide sufficient services, but the population density of skid row is so great that the homeless are forced to migrate to other parts of the city. It is this process of social disaffiliation, greater population density of skid row areas, and limited services that has moved the skid row life far beyond skid row.

DEFINITIONS

"Homelessness" can have several different connotations. It can simply refer to a lack of one's own stable residence where one can sleep and receive mail (Ropers & Robertson 1984a). A broader sociological definition of homelessness may include a recognition of the quality of interactions and of material and social supports a person has. H. Bahr and T. Caplow (1974) include in their definition of homelessness "detachment from society characterized by the absence or attenuation of the affiliation bonds that link settled persons to a network of interconnected social interactions" (p. 55). For Donald J. Bogue (1963), to be homeless is "to live outside private households and have no family life" (p. 2).

That homelessness involves more than simply not having some kind of roof over one's head was also recognized by Samuel Wallace in his important work on the homeless in 1965.

According to Wallace, a person "is still called homeless even though he has a home on skid row" (p. 144).

Poverty expert and political activist Michael Harrington has pointed out that "a 'home' is not simply a roof over one's head. It is the center of a web of human relationships. When the web is shredded as a result of social and economic trends a person is homeless even if he or she has an anonymous room somewhere" (1984, p. 101).

Psychiatrist Leona Bachrach, in a review of research on the homeless mentally ill, concludes that "it is widely agreed that homelessness implies both a lack of shelter and a dimension of disaffiliation or social isolation" (1984, p. 915).

The HUD (1984) study of homelessness proposed the following definition:

> For purposes of this study, then, a person is counted as homeless if his/her night time residence is: (a) in public or private emergency shelters which take a variety of forms—armories, schools, church basements, government buildings, former firehouses and, where temporary vouchers are provided by private or public agencies, even hotels, apartments, or boarding homes; or (b) in the streets, parks, subways, bus terminals, railroad stations, airports, under bridges or aqueducts, abandoned buildings without utilities, cars, trucks, or any other public or private space that is not designed for shelter.
>
> Residents of half-way houses, congregate living facilities, and long-term detoxification centers are not classified as homeless because of the longer-term nature of such facilities. Furthermore, upon discharge, many residents of such facilities will probably not end up on the streets. However, persons who are temporarily in jails or hospitals, but whose usual night time residence is (a) or (b) above, are considered homeless.
>
> While some people are chronically homeless by the above definition, others are homeless on a temporary or episodic basis for a variety of reasons. For example, an elderly person living in a single-room occupancy (SRO) hotel whose sole income is SSI payments may deplete

his/her resources by the third week of the month and live in a shelter until the next check comes, at which time he/she can return to the hotel. Or as noted earlier, a 20 year old single male living at home, or with friends, may move to the streets or shelters occasionally as conditions within the home worsen. Or, an unemployed family may live temporarily in their car until employment is found (p. 8).

It is important that those who are without "shelter," that is, those literally living in the streets, not be substituted for all those who are "homeless." The traditional skid row homeless of the post-World War II period (1945–1970) were basically "sheltered" in SRO hotels or rescue missions. Nevertheless, the wealth of research and literature on this population correctly viewed them as homeless in a sociological sense. What is different about some subpopulations of the homeless in the 1980s is that many of them are not even sheltered in elementary ways.

The "street" homeless—the bag ladies, the shopping cart people, the cardboard box people, and the obviously psychologically wounded—are only the tip of the iceberg. The homeless population itself is stratified relative to the degree of material and social supports a homeless person or family has. At the top of the homeless stratification system are the invisible homeless, those who are temporarily "doubling up" with friends or relatives and those living in SRO hotels; in the middle are the homeless living in working vehicles or emergency shelters; while at the very bottom are those literally in the streets and alleys, trash bins, and cardboard boxes.

TYPOLOGY

See Figure 5.2 for a typology of homeless persons. Generalizations about the homeless population can be made, as for age, race, and employment status, but it may be more useful for social policy to distinguish the different needs of subpopulations among the homeless. They can be classified by demographic characteristics as well as by duration of homelessness.

FIGURE 5.2
A Typology of the Homeless

Definitions of Homeless

1. *Long-Term*	2. *Episodic*	3. *Transitional*
No present residence[1]*	No present residence	No present, stable residence
Homeless more than twelve months	Homeless less than twelve months	Homeless less than twelve months
	At least one previous episode of homelessness	No history of homelessness

*Factors Precipitating Homelessness[2]**	*Estimated Percentage*
Economic/Political	50
Recent impoverishment	
Eviction	
Foreclosure	
Welfare cuts	
Underemployment	
Unemployment	
Retirement	
Political exile	
Immigration	
Migration	
Refugee status	
Undocumented worker status	
Personal	20
Divorce	
Death in family	
Illness or disability	
Domestic violence	
Running away	

*[1] Residence indicates one's own place to sleep and receive mail.

*[2] An individual in any major group may become homeless due to a combination of precipitating factors.

Psychiatric	25
Deinstitutionalization	
Mentally illness	
Retardation	
Drug or alcohol dependence	
Catastrophic	5
Flood	
Fire	
Earthquake	

Subtypes are also identifiable by the event or events causing them to become homeless.

The duration of homelessness is an important factor that influences the intensity of the effect on an individual's physical and mental health. Homeless persons are classified into three major groups using duration as a criterion: long-term, episodic, and transitional. The possible negative effects of repeated or long-term homelessness may include a decline in physical and mental health and increasing difficulty of reentry to the job and housing markets because of diminished mental and physical capacity.

The medical and psychiatric needs of the transitional and episodic homeless, as well as their requirements for occupational adjustment and shelter, differ from those of the long-term homeless. Individuals who become homeless from economic, political or natural factors beyond their control, such as unemployment, evictions, fires, and floods, primarily need financial assistance and temporary shelter, job counseling, and psychological crisis intervention.

Intense psychological intervention, as well as emergency material aid and shelter, are needed by homeless persons suffering from severe mental health problems, physical disabilities, or drug and alcohol dependence and those caught up in temporary personal crises such as divorce or separation, domestic violence, or death in the family.

Several years ago, Susan Sontag wrote in *Illness as a Metaphor* (1979) that society sometimes deals metaphorically with illness when it cannot confront it directly. More recently, Bachrach (1984) indicated that users of data from studies on homelessness should take care not to make a metaphor of mental illness among the homeless mentally ill. One must recognize that psychiatric illness is a major problem in the lives of these individuals, but it is unfortunate that the term "homeless" in the views of many health professionals and the lay public has too often come to mean "mentally ill." This substitution is a result of mass media stereotypes, of the strong advocacy of psychiatrists, and of the fact that some of the most visible homeless are those who appear "mentally ill."

Chapter 6

INSTITUTIONALIZING HOMELESSNESS

Return to the Poorhouses

In 1844, Friedrich Engels described the conditions under which some of the homeless of London were sheltered at night.

> The luckiest of this multitude, those who succeed in keeping a penny or two until evening, enter a lodging-house, such as abound in every great city, where they find a bed. But what a bed! These houses are filled with beds from cellar to garret, four, five, six beds in a room; as many as can be crowded in. Into every bed four, five, or six human beings are piled, as many as can be packed in, sick and well, young and old, drunk and sober, men and women, just as they come, indiscriminately. Then come strife, blows, wounds, or, if these bedfellows agree, so much the worse; thefts are arranged and things done which our language, grown more humane than our deeds, refuses to record (1973, p. 71).

In 1890 Jacob Riis studied the homeless of New York City and the types of "lodging-houses" that existed then to shelter them. Riis uncovered a stratified sheltering system, at the top of which were twenty-five-cent "rooms" and at the bottom, seven-cent beds. Riis described this stratified shelter system in the following way:

> The twenty-five cent lodging-house keeps up the pretence of a bedroom, though the head-high partition enclosing a space just large enough to hold a cot and a chair and allow the man room to pull off his clothes is the shallowest of all pretences. The fifteen-cent bed stands boldly forth without screen in a room full of bunks with sheets as yellow and blankets as foul. At the ten-cent level the locker for the sleeper's clothes disappears. There is no longer need of it. The tramp limit is reached, and there is nothing to lock up save, on general principles, the lodger (1890, pp. 86–87).

Based on police figures, Riis calculated that "the total of the homeless army was 5,121,659" a year who were sheltered in "lodging-houses" in the 1890s. In addition, 69,111 women per year were "lodgers" in police stations (1890, p. 89).

In a 1985 *New York Times* article, "In a Hotel for Homeless Families, Childhood Dies Young," Crystal Nix reported that New York City uses about 57 hotels to house homeless families. In the Holland Hotel, on 42nd Street between Eighth and Ninth Avenues, the city houses 272 homeless families. A one-bedroom apartment costs $60 a day, or about $1,800 a month, and a two-bedroom apartment goes for $100 a day, or about $3,000 a month. The city and state of New York pay 25 percent of the cost, and the federal government pays the remainder. Nix described the Holland Hotel in the following gripping way:

> Children hung from fire escapes and shared the narrow, littered hallways with drug dealers at 3 o'clock in the morning. The sound of gunfire carried into the rooms from the street below. Mothers called to their children to keep away from the half-lighted hallways.
>
> Water dripped from leaky pipes without stop from a stained bathtub in their 11th-floor, two-room apartment.

> The rug was dirty, and the plaster on bare, white walls was peeling. The hotel room was hot and cramped and the furnishings were sparse: one dresser, a television set, two single beds, a chair and a small refrigerator. There is also a hot plate, which is prohibited, for cooking.
>
> At night, there are mice (1985a).

It has been estimated that in 1987 families with children made up 63 percent of New York City's homeless population (United States Conference of Mayors, 1987, p. 5).

Los Angeles County has a kind of public shelter system, like New York City, in that the county gives out emergency housing vouchers to those who qualify. These vouchers are used by homeless individuals to get a room in a single room occupancy (SRO) hotel in skid row. One homeless man described his experience with the voucher system in the following way:

> Almost a month ago I was homeless. I went to the County for help. They gave me a voucher to the Roma Hotel, 510-1/2 So. Main Street. I am in Room 206.
>
> There is no heat, not even a heater or radiator in my room. They gave me one thin blanket, not even big enough to cover my shoulders and feet at the same time. I sleep with a sweater tied around my feet to keep warm. It is just as cold in my room as it is outside. To sleep at all I curl up like a baby does.
>
> I have been sick since I have been in the Roma. I sleep very little. I wake up shivering. I asked for another blanket; the manager said they furnish nothing, not even toilet paper, let alone a blanket.
>
> The first week I was at the Roma, I told the social worker, Ms. Cochran. She said there was nothing she could do about it. I told another social worker—the one who gave me the voucher—I had no heat. She said "Your only other choice is the streets."
>
> I have been looking for a job every day. They won't give me a clothing voucher. I look like hell. I have one jacket. I sleep in it to keep warm. I have been to more

than 20 places looking for work. People look at me, my clothing, my runny nose. They tell me to get lost. It isn't right. I want to work, even though I'm sick. It isn't right to keep me freezing at night in the Roma (Paris, 1984).

Los Angeles also has a private-sector shelter system; two-thirds of these shelters require either some kind of religious counseling or participation in religious activity. In December 1983, the estimated average number of homeless persons sheltered in private emergency shelters in Los Angeles was 1,689, or 4.9 percent of HUD's low estimate of 33,800 (Robertson, Ropers, & Boyer, 1984, p. 61).

Most of the private shelters have exclusionary criteria for admittance, such as no manifestation of mental illness, alcohol or drug abuse, or homosexual behavior. Many shelters allow only a stay of one night, and some require homeless residents to perform work. The largest shelter in Los Angeles only has 200 beds but allows up to 600 homeless persons, in the winter, to sit up in plastic chairs all night.

In 1984 HUD pointed out that "surprisingly little is known about the nature and extent of the effort to assist homeless people in the United States (p. 34). The HUD study reported that only 111,000 persons could be accommodated on any given night in emergency shelters. However, 12,000 of these beds were for runaway youths and another 8,000 were domestic violence beds, leaving only 91,000 for all other homeless individuals. This means that two-thirds of HUD's conservative estimate of 250,000–300,000 homeless were going without shelter.

Additional evidence indicating that today's homeless are recent arrivals on the homeless scene is provided by the fact that 41 percent of all shelters have been in existence four years or less, with 26 percent in existence less than a year (U.S. House Committee on Governmental Operations, 1985, p. 34). In Los Angeles County, as of 1985, 55 percent of the emergency shelters had come into being in the previous five years. While many of these shelters provide meals and showers, some only provide cots, chairs, or spaces on the floor to sleep. Often those accommodated must vacate the premises at extremely early morning hours and are not permitted back until dinner-time.

In 1986 the national demand for emergency shelter increased in 96 percent of the cities surveyed by the United States Conference of Mayors. The average increase in demand for shelter in these cities was 20 percent, and not a single city indicated a decrease in demand. Families with children needing emergency shelter were reported on the rise in 80 percent of the cities (1986, p. 15).

In the face of this growing demand for emergency shelter, 72 percent of the cities surveyed indicated that homeless people were being turned away because of a lack of space and resources. (See Table 6.1.) On the average, 24 percent of the demand for shelter goes unmet (United States Conference of Mayors, 1986, p. 23).

Although emergency shelter cannot be expected to serve as a long-term solution to the homelessness problem, unless we intend to "institutionalize" homelessness as a permanent feature of our society, the immediate needs of the homeless can at least be partially met by increasing the availability of emergency shelter.

Three major types of "sheltering" are currently available to a minority of the homeless. First, there are the temporary emergency shelters, which provide a day or two of refuge from the weather and the hassles of the streets. Often these emergency shelters are little better than human "warehouses." In Dickensian style, homeless individuals who pass the entrance criteria get a cot, a meal, and maybe a shower and then spend the night packed in with many others, usually allowing no private space.

Transitional shelters or special needs shelters are a step up. These shelters are usually targeted for families with children or single mothers with children or in some cases for the mentally ill and drug and alcohol dependent. Counseling or other psychological support is likely in transitional shelters, and in some cases, private rooms and an extended stay of several weeks is provided. Unfortunately, across the nation, very few transitional shelters have been established.

A third type of shelter is characterized as "long-term

TABLE 6.1
Demand for Shelter, 1986

City	Increase in Demand for Emergency Shelter (percentage)	Increase in Families with Children (percentage)	People Turned Away
Boston	—	—	yes
Charleston	—	—	yes
Chicago	8	8	yes
Cleveland	8	13	yes
Denver	20	15	yes
Detroit	—	40	no*
Hartford	—	—	yes
Kansas City	—	34	yes
Los Angeles	50	30	yes
Louisville	—	46	yes
Minneapolis	30	—	no
Nashville	—	—	yes
New Orleans	25	25	yes
New York City	24	20	no
Norfolk	10	20	yes
Philadelphia	25	28	no
Phoenix	25	25	yes
Portland	10	10	no
Salt Lake City	20	29	no*
San Antonio	7	5	no
San Francisco	15	20	yes
San Juan	—	—	yes
Seattle	25	30	yes
Trenton	15	20	yes
Yonkers	15	15	yes

Source: Adapted from *The Continued Growth of Hunger, Homelessness and Poverty in America's Cities* (Washington, DC: United States Conference of Mayors, 1986, p. 28.
*Referral systems have been established to handle overflow.

housing." Single room occupancy (SRO) hotels are a typical example of this kind of sheltering. In many cities, such as Los Angeles, city welfare vouchers are issued to those few homeless who qualify, which can be exchanged for a room in an SRO. Many individuals who live on low fixed incomes rent SRO rooms for most of each month until their money runs out. Then they become street homeless for a period.

Although the decline of the national SRO housing stock has contributed to the increased numbers of street homeless, attempting to preserve and upgrade the remaining SROs is a strategy full of contradictions. There is no doubt that attempting to maintain the present SRO housing stock is an important stop-gap measure, given existing conditions and trends. But preserving SRO housing also contributes to "institutionalized" homelessness in the old traditional skid row flophouse style. The creation of a residentially segregated permanent underclass in skid row areas is not a just or effective long-term solution.

Amazingly, there are some "experts" who feel that too much emphasis is being placed on providing shelter for the homeless. For example, psychiatrist H. Richard Lamb contends,

> There is currently much emphasis on providing emergency shelters to the homeless, and certainly this must be done. But it is important to put the "shelter approach" into perspective; it is a necessary stopgap, symptomatic measure, but does not address the basic causes of homelessness. Too much emphasis on shelters can only delay our coming to grips with the underlying problems that result in homelessness (1984b, p. 58).

The basic cause of homelessness, according to Lamb (see Chapter 4), is chronic mental illness. However, scientific knowledge, as well as simple common sense, tells us that all the psychiatric intervention in the world cannot stabilize an individual unless the individual first has a stable and secure residence. There can also be no doubt that the physical and psychological consequences of homelessness are severe psychosocial stressors, which must be mitigated by food, sleep, shelter, and security.

The private, mostly religious, sector shelters simply do not have the resources to provide for the immediate shelter needs of most of the homeless. Unless there is massive federal assistance, the basic shelter needs of the majority of the homeless will go unfulfilled.

Chapter 7

THE FIGHT BACK

Litigation and Political Struggle

By the mid-1980s, the problem of homelessness was recognized as one of America's leading social problems. Despite this recognition, no coherent national response has been made by the federal government or most local governments. Instead, the issue of homelessness, while increasingly acknowledged, has become intensely politicized.

Because competing political and economic philosophies and policies understand the origin of the current homeless problem in conflicting terms, and because there is great resistance, among conservatives and liberals alike, to overcoming stereotypes and accepting the empirical evidence regarding who the new urban homeless are, there has been little consensus or concerted action to help the homeless. The conservative fiscal policy of the Reagan administration and its subsequent cutbacks and rollbacks in social welfare and housing progams have also made it extremely difficult to deal effectively with the homeless problem.

That the socioeconomic processes discussed in previous chapters have occurred in the same era as the rise of the contemporary homeless is no coincidence. The relationship between these processes and homelessness is supported by the empirical profiles gained from the research. The new urban homeless are essentially the disenfranchised—those who are denied the opportunity to work, denied access to decent low-income housing, and denied access to medical and social aid.

LEGAL STRATEGIES

Litigation has been used both as an advocacy tool and as an instrument to gain immediate relief for the homeless. Outstanding examples of such litigation have taken place in Los Angeles. This chapter will detail several important Los Angeles legal cases.

In one of the first contemporary legal suits on behalf of the homeless, the landmark New York City case of Callahan v. Carey, filed in October 1979, a class of homeless persons established their statutory and constitutional right to shelter; by December 1979 the New York Supreme Court ordered a preliminary injunction making New York City responsible for providing shelter to homeless men (Hopper & Cox, 1982, p. 13). New York City responded by opening a deserted psychiatric hospital building called the Keener Building. However, the city provided no professional supervision, and violence and neglect soon prevailed. In subsequent litigation, the city was forced to provide professional staffing and additional emergency shelters. Nevertheless, additional litigation was in process in 1987 because the warehousing nature of these shelters still did not meet the qualitative standards of decency set forth in the court decision, such as an end to overcrowding, sufficient shower and toilet facilities, and adequate staffing and security.

Up until mid-1984, the County of Los Angeles dealt with homeless persons who qualified by issuing vouchers that could be exchanged for a room in a rundown single room occupancy (SRO) hotel, primarily located in the downtown skid row area. For example, during January 1984, on average, 1,211 persons each night were accommodated in SRO hotels by county vouchers (Robertson, Ropers, & Boyer, 1984, p. 46). When the available spaces in SRO hotels, which held contracts with the county, were exhausted, the county would issue $8 emergency housing checks. Between February and April 1984 the average daily number of checks issued was 50 (Robertson, Ropers, & Boyer, 1984, p. 46).

Allan Heskin of UCLA's Graduate School of Architecture and Urban Planning completed a study of costs and vacancy rates in low-cost hotels and motels in Los Angeles County during the week of 7 May 1984 and concluded,

> This research established that there is virtually no possibility that a person whose only resource is a County warrant in the amount of $8 will actually find shelter in the hotel/motel market in Los Angeles. This is the case primarily because there are virtually no vacancies in those relatively few hotels and motels with rates in the designated range (1984).

In addition, various restrictions existed regarding eligibility for receiving a housing voucher or emergency housing check. Identification was required to be eligible for this form of relief, and even then there was often a waiting period of several days before any assistance was given. Homeless persons often lack IDs because they have lost all their belongings or had them stolen, along with their IDs. Those applying for emergency shelter often became homeless because of the waiting period before they could receive assistance.

In reaction to these barriers to immediate assistance and on behalf of the homeless in general, the Homeless Litigation Team, composed of attorneys from six public-interest law firms, filed a suit (Eisenheim v. County Board of Supervisors) against the County of Los Angeles demanding that the ID requirement and the waiting period be removed as barriers to aid. In December 1983 Los Angeles County was ordered by a Superior Court judge to cease these practices.

A second lawsuit (Ross v. County Board of Supervisors) was filed regarding the insufficiency of the $8 emergency lodging checks to actually provide shelter. In August 1984 the county was enjoined from issuing these checks. The county responded by increasing the rates paid to SRO hotels by 45 percent without improving the quality of the accommodations. Within three months the number of hotels participating in this program increased from 77 to 151 (Blasi, 1984, p. 6).

The private owners of SRO voucher hotels were making as much as $15,000 a month from the vouchers, and at least one hotel owner made nearly a million dollars during the year. Investigations by Legal Aid found most of these hotels in violation of fire, safety, and health codes and in some cases found that long-term SRO tenants were being evicted so the hotels could become county voucher hotels. As a consequence of these findings, a third lawsuit was filed to stop taxpayer funds from supporting those hotels that were in open violation of the health, safety, and fire laws (Paris, 1984).

On 8 June 1984, in a different legal case, Los Angeles Municipal Court Judge Ronald Schoenberg found Penny Benjamin, a homeless, unemployed housekeeper, not guilty of violating L.A. municipal code 85.02, which prohibits habitating in a vehicle. The not-guilty verdict was the result of the defense of "necessity." The judge was convinced that Benjamin was forced to violate 85.02, out of necessity because she was homeless and unemployed. While this ruling did not set a legal precedent, nor overturn 85.02, it may influence the disposition of other cases. Benjamin was defended by K. Wolfe of the Legal Aid Foundation of Los Angeles.

The Los Angeles County Department of Public Social Services has a cash welfare program called *general relief* (GR). The GR basic allowance for one person living alone was $228 per month in 1985. This welfare program is intended for individuals who are not eligible for other cash welfare programs and who are destitute. Nonetheless, a lawsuit was filed against Los Angeles County (Bannister, 1985) claiming that the GR "60-day penalty" provision actually caused some poor people to become homeless. Individuals in the process of applying for or receiving GR could be placed on "60-day penalty" (denied GR for 60 days) as punishment for various infractions of welfare regulations or for disobeying the oral directives of welfare workers. In 1985 an average of 2,500 persons were put on the "60-day penalty" each month. Missing an appointment or being late for an appointment with a case worker, not completing the required monthly 20 job searches, or "tardy" documentation or refusal to take an assigned work project were some of the grounds for receiving the "60-day penalty." The county justification of this penalty was to provide GR applicants with "incentive" and "to encourage self-respect and self-reliance and to develop and maintain good work habits."

The reality, however, was that putting someone out on the streets for 60 days did nothing for the individual's work ethic and only moved that person further away from being employed and finding permanent shelter. As a result of the suit against the "60-day penalty," the county was ordered to be more prudent and selective in its implementation.

In another suit brought against Los Angeles County, the Homeless Litigation Team provided evidence that the mentally and developmentally disabled indigent and homeless residents of Los Angeles are effectively excluded from GR because of an "exceedingly and unnecessarily complex and convoluted application process" (Rensch, 1986). Citing the testimony of expert witnesses, the litigation team contended that the GR application was intentionally discriminatory. In their brief, for example, they quoted Robert Chaffee, former director of the Bureau of Assistance Payments, Department of Public Social Services, Los Angeles County, as stating, "The welfare application process . . . was designed to be rough. It is designed, quite frankly, to be exclusionary" (Rensch, 1986).

Many of the homeless who suffer from the debilitating psychological and physical consequences of unemployment and homelessness and those homeless who suffer from chronic mental disorders were denied the last hope of emergency welfare relief because they could not negotiate the hurdles of the welfare bureaucracy. The county was ordered to provide more assistance during the application process for those homeless who were deemed mentally disabled.

In yet another suit regarding GR (Blair, 1985), it was alleged that the monthly grant of $228, of which $143 is supposedly allotted to housing, was insufficient to secure the basic necessities of life in Los Angeles and resulted in "enforced homelessness" of thousands of GR recipients. Evidence was submitted demonstrating that no housing of any kind was available in Los Angeles for $143 per month. Consequently, many homeless GR recipients had to utilize the nonhousing allotment to supplement the $143 housing allotment. By doing so, they were using up the remainder of their $228, grant, which was intended for the other necessities of life. As a result of the Blair suit, as of 1 July 1987 the County of Los Angeles was to adjust its GR monthly allowance from $247 to $312 over a two-year period.

More recent litigation is a direct result of city efforts to "clean up" wooden and cardboard box settlements on the streets and in vacant lots, which are preferred by many of the urban homeless to the vermin-infested and unsafe SRO hotels.

A series of "sweeps" in early 1987 were carried out against the communities of homeless citizens. After a 10-minute warning given by the police, city sanitation workers scooped up the makeshift wooden and cardboard box "homes," portable toilets and all personal belongings. Los Angeles City officials considered such "shantytowns" as havens for crime and disease and simply an embarrassment for Los Angeles. Mayor Tom Bradley, according to the *Los Angeles Times*, claimed responsibility for the sweeps and justified them as part of a skid row clean-up campaign (Clifford & Clayton, 1987). A Bradley official, Andrew Raubeson, head of the Los Angeles SRO Housing Corporation, went along with the police to aid in conducting the sweeps.

One of the homeless victims of the "clean up" described what happened.

> My name is Rachel and I am 37 years old. I was born in Pasadena and raised in L.A. I graduated from Garfield High School.
>
> I've been living on Towne Ave. for three months with my husband. We had constructed a wooden "house," that was pretty stable and met our needs. I had plates and all the necessities. We had a mattress, blankets and sleeping bags. We had pots and pans, clothing and personal items.
>
> Wednesday morning I got up, got dressed, went to the potty and went back and told David to get up and not

forget to do his exercises. I told him not to forget to read the Bible, too. I was going to sleep a little more before getting ready for the day.

David poked his head in the house and said, "Hon, they're gonna sweep." I said "Damn" and looked out and started to cry. I knew they were gonna take my house. That house meant a lot to me.

I took off the coverings of the house, rolled up the blankets, and tried to get parts of the house pulled out and ready to take away. Then I tried to help other people in our community.

I tried to help people with their carts, to get the baskets up onto the sidewalk to load up the carts.

Our kitchen was all set up. I helped grab a bag of onions. Everything went into the streets—rice, salt and pepper, noodles, utensils, storage cabinets, glassware, stone containers, some new frills we'd just gotten and a lot of donations of clothing. I just stood and watched.

A woman who regularly comes down to give us donations, came in the middle of it, to leave some things for us. We told her not to leave things because all the things were being dumped out.

County workers, probably G.R. work project people, came down and put everything, everything in the gutters.

We all have hopes and dreams. I do. When I saw them throwing away pieces of wood that were my house, I felt like my hopes and dreams were there in the gutter. David had built that house. It meant a lot to me. It's just very personal. Now that house is gone.

Bulldozers came down the street and put all the peoples' things in the dumpster down by Fred Jordan's. I told my friend, Sandra, on the corner, to whom this had happened before, now I knew how she felt. Just sick inside.

G.R. doesn't give sufficient monetary grant to live on. Here I don't have roaches, rats, people busting in my door. Here I have neighbors, we're family. I just want to live a normal life. This is America. I'm determined; this is most important to me. I may be off the track, so to speak, but I'm still a human being (Bennion, 1987).

The Reverend Don Kribs observed some of the homeless "sweeps" and thought they resembled the treatment of the poor in Third World cultures. Kribs, the head of the Peace and Justice Committee of the Council of Priests for the Archdiocese of Los Angeles, described what he saw.

On the morning of Feb. 23, 1987, I assembled with other members of the clergy at the corner of 5th St. and Central in downtown Los Angeles. I was there to observe the sweeps of homeless people that were being carried out by city officials, the police and local merchants. On the corner I saw at least 5 police cars, several dump trucks, a skip loader, and several trucks filled with men with push brooms.

The process was very dehumanizing for the people on the street who were the object of the operation. The token effort of one representative of Traveller's Aid (the only service organization actually participating in the sweep) to both announce the sweep and offer mission referrals was of no practical value to the homeless people since all of the missions are full. The representative of Traveller's Aid also was obviously being used to give the outward appearance of respectability, care and concern to the whole operation.

It was clear that the sweep was being orchestrated by the business community because the Central City East Association representative, Laurie Flack, was telling the police which homeless groups to remove from the sidewalks.

I have seen similar operations carried out against the poor and homeless in El Salvador and I am ashamed to see this happening in my own country.

The sweep began when the caravan of police and city vehicles moved to the corner of 6th and Stanford. There were two encampments of homeless people on two different street corners, one north of 6th St. and one south of 6th St. The Traveller's Aid representative announced it to the other group. The dump trucks, skip loader and sweepers destroyed the 2nd encampment before the Traveller's

Aid representative had a chance to talk to any of the people. When he did talk to the homeless people in the first camp, he did not hand out literature, but simply gave verbal referrals to the missions and to his office. Many of the people from the second camp scattered before he had an opportunity to talk to them.

I did not hear the police announce any statement of rights or inform the homeless people of what laws were being violated prior to the beginning of the sweep and removal of possessions.

The homeless people were given only several minutes warning of the sweep before the trucks moved in to destroy the camps. A number of the people could not carry all of their belongings away with them and had to leave them on the sidewalk to be removed by the city trucks.

The second sweep followed the procedures used in the first sweep and took place on the Southeast corner of 5th and San Pedro Streets.

These sweeps have been advertised to the community as a way to get rid of crime and drug dealing. But from my pastoral work of many years in this area I know that it is not the encampments of the homeless that are the problem, but that drug dealing is allowed to continue openly and unabated by the police on street corners downtown. This reinforces my belief that the primary purpose of these sweeps is to pacify the local business community and not to control crime or provide real shelter options for the homeless. I did not observe any arrests being made or drugs being confiscated during these raids that I have described.

It was very disturbing to watch this scenario being carried out here in the United States of America (Bennion, 1987).

On 10 March 1987, Los Angeles Board of Public Works President Maureen Kindel led a procession of officials on an inspection of skid row shantytowns and then condemned them for "health and safety" reasons just before city crews dismantled them (Carlson, 1987a).

A suit to prevent further sweeps was filed by the American Civil Liberties Union, and later the Homeless Litigation Team joined the suit. As a result, an injunction was issued requiring the city to give 12-hour notice to the homeless before a sweep takes place (Blasi, 1987).

The lawsuits described here have resulted not only in providing immediate relief for many of the homeless, but also in increasing the attention from the public and private sectors because of the publicity given to the plight of the homeless in the mass media.

PROTEST MOVEMENTS

Like prerevolutionary Russian Cossacks tramping through the villages of terrified peasants, the Los Angeles mounted police first began the downtown raids against the homeless described as "hype sweeps" during the summer of 1984, when Los Angeles played host to the international Olympic games. In an attempt to "sanitize" the downtown area, 30 equestrian police officers were assigned to roust the most visible of the homeless, disperse them, and thus "polish" the city's image for the Olympic visitors. Attorneys for the homeless filed several claims against the police for illegal search and seizure during this period and contended that for months prior to the Olympics, rumors were widespread regarding impending largescale arrests of the homeless (Roderick, 1984).

Out of this context of intimidation and lack of any public emergency shelter for one of the largest homeless populations in the nation, the homeless themselves began to organize and fight back politically with what newspapers claimed looked like a "battlefield hospital"; the homeless preferred to call it Tent City. Within the shadow of Los Angeles City Hall, on a small, grassy, state-owned lot, over 200 homeless men and women, with the help of volunteers, erected two huge tents to serve as temporary shelters and to dramatize their plight during the Christmas season of 1984 (Dolan, 1984).

The volunteers were led by the Homeless Organizing Team, whose members are paralegals, social workers, and independent political activists. Tent City was erected on December 18, partially as an attempt to draw public attention to the county's 60-day penalty, which the organizers hoped to have reduced or removed. Tent City was scheduled to be dismantled on December 26, by state order, but a one-week extension was granted by the state because of the "spirit of the holiday season" and because officials viewed the "gathering" as orderly (Hernandez & Wolinsky, 1984).

On Wednesday, 2 January 1985, Tent City was dismantled and the homeless cleared out. As this was taking place, the Los Angeles County Board of Supervisors was meeting to decide the fate of the 60-day penalty. In attendance at that meeting were about 80 homeless people. When the board declined to change the penalty, about a dozen homeless individuals refused to leave the building. They bound themselves together and chanted, "All we are saying is give us a home!" At 6 PM, 13 homeless protesters were arrested and dragged away from the building to jail. Among them was a charismatic black man, Ted Hayes (Connell & Dolan, 1985).

Five months later, in May 1985, a new phenomenon emerged in the contemporary homeless situation. Reminiscent of the shantytowns called Hoovervilles during the depression of the 1930s, a group of homeless in Los Angeles created a community of cardboard box and plywood huts that they dubbed Justiceville. Justiceville was more than an attempt to protect its residents from the elements; it became a real community, with a division of labor and a sense of sharing, caring, and solidarity.

Sociologically Justiceville would come to represent a case study in "empowerment," an attempt by the homeless to provide themselves with the shelter, community, and dignity denied them by their social system.

Milton Meltzer, in his book *Brother Can You Spare a Dime*, wrote about new forms of "housing" developed during the depression of the 1930s.

> Unemployment became a way of life, and out of it developed a new style of housing. There was no money for rent. The homeless could make only short stays in the

shelters supported by the city or private charity. Unemployed men began to create their own shelters wherever
they could find unused land. New York City was soon
sprinkled with new settlements (1969, p. 87).

Once again, as unemployment and homelessness reached
epidemic proportions in the 1980s, the homeless began to
create their own communities. But this time a political dimension to the shantytowns developed at a very early stage.

Ted Hayes emerged as the primary leader and organizer
of Justiceville. Hayes, a former minister once active in the civil
rights and student protests of the 1960s, was one of a tiny
minority of the homeless to "choose" to be homeless. His
motivation was based on his understanding that the issue of
homelessness in the 1980s is one of the most pressing moral
and human rights issues facing the United States.

The site on which Justiceville was erected was a vacant lot
in skid row, which until February 1985 had been leased by the
Catholic Worker Movement as a playground for poor children.
When Hayes came to the site in late January/early February,
there were 10 or 15 homeless squatters there. Soon this community grew to over 60 residents, mostly Black and Hispanic,
and the encampment came to be known as Justiceville.

Under Hayes' leadership, Justiceville became more than
just a "hobo camp." Hayes and the other residents believed that
Justiceville should also be a moral and political statement and
symbol. As Hayes put it,

> Let's do something about it. Let's change it. Let's not wait
> for them to change it because we've been waiting for years.
> Black people have been waiting for 400 years for them to
> change it, and they haven't. Hispanics have been waiting.
> Indians, poor whites have been waiting for years, and they
> haven't done it. In fact, it has gotten worse (Hayes, 1985).

By April city officials were preparing to have Justiceville
removed. Claiming unsanitary conditions, the city condemned
it as a health hazard. Justiceville was given a reprieve from the
Health Department eviction order on 17 April, and plans were

made to solicit for portable toilets and running water (Edelstein, 1985). Four Port-a-Johns were donated 1 May by private sanitation companies, and Justiceville was now able to solve it's most pressing public health issue—disposal of human waste.

While controversy surrounded the issue of whether Justiceville was a viable self-help shelter alternative model for the homeless, there was no doubt that by the spring of 1985 through intensive mass media coverage, Justiceville had become a rallying symbol of hope and dignity for the Los Angeles homeless and the general public had become more aware of the issue of homelessness. Nonetheless, less than two weeks after the portable toilets were installed, the city moved in with bulldozers to raze Justiceville. Lois Arkin, director of the Cooperative Resources and Services Project of Los Angeles, submitted a petition to Mayor Bradley's office to delay for 60 days any attempt to close down Justiceville, but the petition was unsuccessful (Ackerman, 1985).

At 8 AM on 10 May 1985, a 14-officer task force headed by Captain Bill Wedgeworth of the Los Angeles Police Department Central Division, gave notice to Justiceville residents to leave or be arrested. Singing "We Shall Overcome," 11 residents, including Hayes, refused to leave and were arrested and hauled off to jail in a police bus. Other residents were offered shelter in various emergency shelters, but most returned to the streets (Carison, 1985).

The following day, 11 May, Justiceville was razed to the ground by city bulldozers. The city's justification was that Justiceville faced six counts of health violation charges. Ted Hayes had a different interpretation.

> Oh, they just said sanitation was the main issue. . . . So, we got toilets put in. We cleaned it out ourselves, put up a wall, put sand in it and had the toilets brought in. The supervisor came back, said, "OK you are not breaking the law anymore by urinating and defecating on the streets, but it's illegal to have these toilets here." I mean, we were damned if we don't, damned if we do. I think it was more the idea that we were trying to do something for ourselves, and I think we were embarrassing the system (Hayes, 1985).

The charges against Hayes and the other members of the Justiceville 11, as they came to be known, had been dropped by May 25. The *Los Angeles Herald*, in an editorial entitled "The Meaning of Justiceville: L.A.'s Homeless Require Shelter and Support," stated, "It stood . . . as a pitiful symbol of the destitute, struggling to care for themselves. The value of Justiceville, and the Tent City before it, is that local government is being drawn into the solution" ("Meaning of Justiceville," 1985).

Hayes and his followers knew they could not count on the city alone to try to "solve" the homeless crisis. Continued agitation and political struggle would be necessary. A march of the homeless and their supporters on Los Angeles City Hall took place May 22. The objective was to maintain the visibility of the plight of the homeless. The march on city hall was followed in a few days by the establishment of Justiceville II. The second community was built on a vacant lot in skid row owned by the Richfield International Management Co. The company's manager, Terry Lee, initially agreed that Hayes's group could utilize the lot, clean it up, clear bushes, and live there until the company was ready to develop the property. But on 3 June 1985, Lee and seven police cars arrived at the site. Hayes, Walter Bannister, and Wendel Grady refused to leave and were arrested for trespassing (Dolcemascolo, 1985).

Tragedy followed in the coming months. Harry Rodgers, a 32-year-old black man, one of the organizers of Justiceville and a Los Angeles legal clinic volunteer, was slain in a skid row soup kitchen line on Tuesday, 27 August 1985. While attempting to break up a fight, Rodgers was stabbed with a knife in the throat (McMillan, 1985).

Over the next several months, Hayes and his followers continued to organize and to be arrested for various crimes, such as sleeping overnight on the grounds of the Los Angeles Music Center. By this time Hayes and the idea of "Justicevilles" springing up all over downtown Los Angeles were evoking strong and mixed reactions. The city and the long-established skid row charity agencies considered Hayes a romantic idealist at best and a dangerous revolutionary at worst.

In the early months of 1986, however, Hayes and his

"tribe," as he began to describe his followers, began to make headway with some elected officials. Richard Alatorre, a new councilman from the 14th District, had been influenced by Hayes to introduce a motion in City Council to open up foyers, parking structures and fallout structures to the Los Angeles homeless. The major opponent of this plan was the Community Redevelopment Agency (CRA), a business-dominated city group whose major goal was to revitalize and gentrify the downtown (Zasada, 1986). The motion did not pass, but ironically some aspects of it became reality a year later.

Meanwhile, the propaganda impact of Justiceville reached a peak with the production of a video entitled *Trouble in Paradise: A Look at L.A.'s Homeless*, which won an Emmy in 1986. The video was produced and directed by Gary Glaser, a recently unemployed and temporarily homeless ex–stage manager at KTLA's "Hour Magazine." Clips from *Trouble in Paradise* were shown in April 1986 on "Hour Magazine," a nationally broadcast talk show (*Trouble in Paradise*, 1985). Glaser went on to produce a longer version in 1987 entitled *Justiceville*.

During 1986, despite the gains of various legal suits brought on behalf of the homeless, the addition of a few hundred private emergency shelter beds, and the enormous amount of mass media coverage, both in Los Angeles and nationally, the ranks of the homeless grew, with no real improvement in their condition.

Hayes, who for months, had been sleeping most of the time in the car garage of the Los Angeles Music Center, started in late 1986 to organize for the establishment of Tent City II. After $2,500 was secured from a private donor for insurance costs, a huge tent and eight smaller ones were erected on 26 December 1986 on a state-owned lot that had been the site of the state office building.

About 200 homeless men, women, and children were encamped there. Marion and John Mosley were two of the residents of Tent City II. As reported in the *Los Angeles Herald Examiner*,

> For the last two months, Marion and John Mosley had been dividing their nights between the streets and door-

ways of downtown Los Angeles and a garage at the Criminal Courts building.

Homeless, virtually penniless, and getting by largely because of the hot meals served at any number of Skid Row missions, the Mosleys were without much hope until Saturday, the day they moved whatever belongings they had to Tent City II.

Life, said the 48-year-old Marion Mosley, "is suddenly looking up. Saturday was the first time in two months I've been able to sleep through the night" (Fink, 1986).

The State of California allowed Tent City II to stay up until 3 January 1987. Hayes and the homeless wanted to keep the site as an ongoing community for and by the homeless.

"It's beyond temporary," said Lillie Smith, 60, a homeless woman. "I'd like some stability before I die."

It's a savage nation of people that will allow elderly, shelterless, disabled people to exist on the streets," she said (Mullen, 1986).

The state, county, and city, which jointly owned the property, had other plans. The county was expecting to begin receiving bids in February "to allow a private developer to build a 20-story commercial building on the site. . . . The developer would be granted a 66-year lease" (Mullen, 1986). It was estimated that $1 billion would be generated in rents for the state, county, and city of Los Angeles.

Once again officials moved to dismantle a homeless community, and once again a confrontation developed between the police and the homeless. Hayes, Paul Robinson, and Susie Foafua were arrested on 6 January 1987 for "battery and interfering with police officers, inciting to riot and disturbing the peace" (Chandler 1987). Later, officials dropped the charges, claiming that "this is just not a good time for prosecuting."

On 25 January 1987 the *Los Angeles Times* reported that "demand for emergency shelter rose 50 percent last year in Los Angeles, the biggest increase in the country." Demand for emergency shelter for families with children also rose by 30 percent ("Homelessness in L.A.," 1987). During the second week of January 1987, four homeless persons died from exposure in the record-breaking cold spell that hit Los Angeles. This prompted the City Council to vote, 10–0, for an unprecedented action: open City Hall to shelter the homeless from the cold. The *Los Angeles Times* described the first person to enter City Hall.

> One of the first to enter was Sylvia Castro, 23, who was carrying her 3-month-old son, Thomas Ricardo, in her arms. She sank down in the place indicated by one of the monitors appointed to arrange sleeping space and leaned her head against a seat.
> "I don't know what's going to become of me," she said.
> She said she and her infant had been on the streets since they left the home for unwed mothers in Long Beach where Thomas Ricardo was born (Simon and Himmel, 1987).

Ted Hayes took charge of security at this City Hall encampment. Meanwhile, Los Angeles Police Chief Darryl F. Gates rejected the city council's request to open Parker Center police station to the homeless as well. Gates called the opening of City Hall to the homeless a "terrible mistake," arguing that this action would draw more homeless people to Los Angeles. He described the homeless as "alcoholics and vagrants" who "are homeless because they choose to be homeless" (Simon & Himmel, 1987).

Los Angeles City Councilman Yaroslavsky compared Gates's statement to the one imputed to Marie Antoinette: "I guess the chief says 'Let them eat blankets'" (Simon & Himmel, 1987). Using City Hall as an emergency shelter lasted only a few days; subsequently the city funded a temporary 1000-bed shelter, which was open only three months. In late June 1987 the city was funding only 150 beds (Blasi, 1987).

In February and March of 1987, other organizations of the homeless began following strategies similar to those of Hayes. The Los Angeles Union of the Homeless, headed by "Mormon Priest" Adam Bennion, started the South Towne settlement, which was razed by the police and city workers in the sweeps described in the litigation discussion above.

Controversy continued to plague Mayor Bradley's policies toward the homeless. At the end of May 1987 a dispute erupted between Police Chief Gates and Los Angeles City Attorney James Hahn. On May 28, Chief Gates announced that the homeless had seven days to get off the streets of the Los Angeles downtown skid row or face arrest. Mayor Bradley endorsed the proposed police sweeps of the street homeless; as Bradley put it, "I support the L.A.P.D.'s plan to clean up Skid Row" (McMillan, 1987a). Chief Gates had little sympathy for the Los Angeles homeless, justifying police sweeps on the grounds that

> The vast majority are there because of their indulgences.
> . . . These people could be given a limousine ride to another area. . . . They'd come right back here. This is where they want to live. . . . My responsibility is to maintain order and peace (McMillan, 1987a).

City Attorney Hahn, however, defied the police chief by indicating he would not prosecute any homeless arrested in police sweeps. As reported by the *Los Angeles Herald Examiner*, Hahn maintained,

> I see my job as a prosecutor as seeing that justice is done, not putting people in jail for sleeping on the streets.
>   Number one, I don't believe I have a prosecutable case. Two, these cases can be very hard to win, to get a jury to convict a man for these offenses. And personally, I don't think it's the right thing to do (Carison, 1987b).

On 2 June 1987 the Los Angeles City Council requested Chief Gates not to arrest the homeless for sleeping on the streets if alternative housing was not available (McMillan, 1987b). The next day Mayor Bradley proposed a temporary (three-month) camp for the homeless on a vacant downtown lot near the Los Angeles River. The proposed "urban campground" would accommodate 600 homeless individuals and be administered by the Salvation Army (Cusolito, 1987).

Despite the attempts to stop police sweeps of the homeless, Los Angeles police officers began a crackdown on sidewalk dwellers on the evening of 4 June 1987. As a compromise, Mayor Bradley ordered the police to offer homeless individuals vouchers for SRO hotels and only to arrest them if they failed to leave or accept a voucher. When the 40 police officers arrived at 6th Street and Stanford Avenue, the site of one of the largest street encampments, they found more news crew members than homeless individuals. The residents of the street encampments had already cleared out, fearful of arrests and of losing their few meager possessions.

Moving through other areas of skid row that evening, the police gave out a total of only 23 vouchers for temporary stays at SRO hotels and arrested three homeless individuals (McMillan and Ramos, 1987).

Bradley's "urban campground," surrounded by a fence and policed by Salvation Army "guards," was labeled by skid row activists and many of the homeless as "a concentration camp for segregating the poor" ("Skid Row Pavilions," 1987). Lillie Smith, a 61-year-old homeless woman, stated, "Mayor Bradley is a joke. Putting up a camp gulag for the homeless—how dare they!" (Prokop, 1987).

By 1987 Hayes had come to personify the homeless movement of Los Angeles. But while he had become the recognized spokesperson of the movement in the mass media, he was only the most visible of the many homeless individuals who were politically struggling on their own behalf. Hayes, understanding that the issue of homelessness and the homeless themselves represent a serious political and ideological threat to the conservative political establishment, expressed his fears in a *Los Angeles Times* profile.

> Either they're going to find some reason to slander me, bad press me . . . or put me away for subverting the security of the United States, something like that. I'll end up in a concentration camp or a jail, or deported, asked to leave the county, or forced underground.

> I'm an American dissident, like the Soviet dissidents.
> . . . I'm afraid of being tortured some day behind the
> scenes where nobody can see it, where there's no evidence
> of torture (Decker, 1987).

In other major U.S. cities, like San Francisco; Santa Barbara; Washington, D.C.; and New York City, homeless political
and direct action struggles continue to be organized and
waged. Like other poor people's movements, the early stages of
the "homeless movement" are characterized by clearly identifiable features. Frances Fox Piven and Richard A. Cloward
(1977) suggest that economic and social dislocations that disrupt the structures and routines of daily life are a necessary
condition for the rise of protest movements (p. 11). Homelessness is, of course, an extraordinary disturbance in the lives
of those affected, and the large-scale economic and social dislocations taking place in the United States in the 1980s (discussed
in Chapter 3) have been disruptive to many other segments of
American society. Nevertheless, while there was some spo-
radic protest among striking workers and farmers in the early
years of the 1980s, major and mass political protest has yet to
emerge.

None, however, are more disenfranchised than the homeless. Not only are they disenfranchised economically and
socially, but in most cities and states, they do not have the right
to vote because they have no fixed addresses. In addition, the
homeless are stigmatized by social welfare services and psychiatric establishments that view them as pathological clients
unable to care for themselves, let alone engage in effective
political struggle for their rights.

The developing protest movements among the homeless in
Los Angeles and elsewhere, despite their current limitations,
are progressing through the expected stages of successful
protest movements. Piven and Cloward (1977) have outlined
the elements entailed in an emerging protest movement: two
major events are necessary for it to be successful, a change in
consciousness and a change in behavior.

The change in consciousness must be realized among the
members of a movement and the segments of society they wish

to influence. Specifically, three dimensions of "consciousness" must be altered: (a) belief in the legitimacy of current arrangements, procedures, structures, and prevailing ideology must be given up; (b) the members of the movement must come to believe that existing arrangements are not fixed or inevitable and thus realize the possibility of asserting their "rights"; and (c) a new sense of efficacy among the members must develop. Groups once thought to be helpless must realize they have the capacity to alter conditions.

These changes in consciousness must then bring about the change in behavior; the movement must become defiant, violating the social expectations and even the laws the members of the movement deem unjust. This defiance must become collective to maximize its effect (Piven & Cloward, 1977, pp. 3–4).

The history of Justiceville has clearly followed these steps. There are, however, definite limitations to the chances for success of homeless movements. Without a major shift in national and local political and social priorities and a linkage of homeless movements with more powerful allies like organized labor or traditional civil rights groups, the best that can be hoped for is a nudge to the public conscience and minor reforms of the welfare system. The psychological and ideological resistance to acknowledging the real causes of homelessness and accepting the reality of the composition of the homeless population also limit the chances that homeless movements can succeed.

Leaders like Ted Hayes obviously have not created the homeless crisis, nor are they individually responsible for the increasing defiance of the homeless. Leaders, whatever their individual motives or idiosyncracies, may come to personify a struggle in the mass media, but unless they are more or less representative of their constituents and the issues, they do not endure or succeed in building a movement.

Chapter 8

REGAINING THE AMERICAN DREAM

Understanding who the homeless are and where they come from must be the first step in proposing strategies to help. Contrary to popular stereotypes, most of the new homeless are not traditional "derelicts" or "bums." The available evidence shows that the new urban homeless are casualties of a crisis in low-income housing, economic change, and political and social policies.

Blacks and other minorities are disproportionately affected by all these factors. As William Wilson, a black sociologist at the University of Chicago, has pointed out regarding the impact on blacks of job loss through deindustrialization,

> You have to look at where the jobs are—not just how many were created. Blacks have borne the brunt of deindustrialization on their heavy concentration in the steel, automobile, rubber and textile industries. If you look at the data on blacks moving out of poverty throughout the 1940s, the 1950s, the 1960s, you see that much of that movement was due to getting higher-paying jobs in the industrial sector. That has all been reversed (1986, p. 21).

Wilson is also one of the few social scientists to recognize that it is primarily the crisis of U.S. industry and its occupational structure, and not the "subculture" of its victims, that is creating an "underclass" of homeless blacks. In this regard, Wilson states,

> Within the lower class is an underclass population, a heterogeneous grouping at the very bottom of the economic class hierarchy. This underclass population includes those lower-class workers whose income falls below the poverty level, the long-term unemployed, discouraged workers who have dropped out of the labor market, and the more or less permanent welfare recipients.
>
> The distinctive characteristics of the underclass are also reflected in the large number of unattached adult males who have no fixed address, who live mainly on the streets, and who roam from one place of shelter to another (1985, p. 172).

One of the first things that needs to be done is to correct public perceptions of the nature of the homeless population. This would include correcting the stereotypes held even by many who provide services to the homeless. Some service providers are still operating with old impressions of the homeless as primarily the white, elderly, alcohol- or drug-dependent "derelicts" of previous decades.

The immediate needs for employment and shelter for the homeless require innovative cooperation between the private and public sectors. The private sector, usually in the form of religious organizations, is extremely limited in its resources. This is why, for example, only 9 percent of the estimated homeless population of Los Angeles County is accommodated with some form of emergency shelter on any given night. Without increased assistance by local and federal governments, private-sector efforts to meet the short-term needs of the homeless for emergency shelter and food will continue to be inadequate.

The long-term needs of the homeless probably will require a reevaluation of national and local political trends and policies. In the present climate, however, with policies of fiscal conservatism regarding social welfare and a reversal of 50 years of governmental support of low-income housing, it is unlikely that political leadership will initiate long-term programs such as massive low-income housing projects, a national jobs program, or increased social welfare.

The solution to the homeless crisis is ultimately political, because the reallocation of resources necessary to provide the homeless with what they need involves the utilization of economic, social, and political power. Nothing less than a major shift in priorities at the federal level will do.

For immediate relief, the President should declare homelessness a national emergency. If as many people were homeless as the result of a flood, an earthquake, or some other natural disaster as are homeless because of national economic trends, the President would not hesitate to provide federal assistance. The same should be done for victims of social, economic, and political upheavals beyond their control as is done for victims of natural disasters.

Emergency shelters, soup kitchens, or outdoor campsites, however, are only short-term "band-aids." Long-term strategies are really needed, to provide solutions that will end homelessness. Reestablishment of an aggressive and effective national housing program for low-income Americans must be a priority. And if the economy continues not to "trickle down" jobs, national public work programs will be necessary. The unemployed could be given work in the construction of low-income housing; in repairing and expanding our cities' streets, highways, and bridges; and in maintaining our national parks, schools, and hospitals. The resources are available; all we need is the will. Finally, the destruction and imposed limitation of our social welfare systems need to be reversed.

The money for all these things could be reallocated from other areas of the federal budget, such as the defense budget. Once the unemployed and homeless have jobs and stable homes, the chances of their mental health improving are greatly enhanced and the benefits of psychological intervention facilitated.

In some cases, however, the homeless are not simply

waiting for others to help them. The homeless in some cities are beginning to organize themselves politically to focus attention on their plight and find some answers. An example of such political activity was the creation of "Justiceville" (see Chapter 7) in early 1985. Until it was dismantled by police, Justiceville was a model of "empowerment" in which mostly nonwhite homeless people attempted to build a community of cardboard boxes and wooden shacks to provide the shelter and dignity denied them by government policy (Carison 1985).

The emergence of a new urban homeless underclass in the United States is essentially a result of growing economic and social inequity. The contemporary homeless, who are disproportionately nonwhite, are victims of massive social and economic dislocation and displacements. Not so long ago, most Americans considered themselves middle class, and the sky was the limit to what they believed they could achieve. The early 1980s witnessed a resurgence of national pride at the very same time that many Americans began to lose ground economically. By the mid-1980s, earlier optimism was clashing with economic and social realities. Record-level unemployment rates, the deindustrialization of American industries, the farm crisis, international trade wars, unstable interest rates, increasing poverty, persistent racial conflict, political crises, and an alarming growth in the number of homeless Americans began to shatter the American Dream for a large segment of the population.

Rather than moving toward greater economic security and unity of national purpose, in the latter part of the 1980s the United States is increasingly becoming a polarized society. The polarization has widened both between social classes and between racial groups. An understanding of the roots of this polarization escapes most Americans, who by and large continue to view social problems in individualistic terms. There is evidence, however, that while consciousness of the origins of our social problems lags behind the impact of the reality of these problems, an increasing number of people are beginning to put two and two together. The way a society responds to those who, for whatever reason, are unable to care for themselves is indicative of a number of things; the health of its economy and its national spirit and the nature and direction of its priorities are at least to some extent reflected in the way it treats its most helpless members.

The homeless symbolize a malfunctioning of major social institutions and perhaps a malaise of community spirit. Our social institutions function as if we had first-class, coach, and economy rules and rewards for different segments of the population.

In his keynote speech before the 1984 Democratic Convention, New York Governor Mario Cuomo suggested that a more fitting metaphor of the nation's condition than Reagan's "Shining City on a Hill" was "A Tale of Two Cities." Cuomo explained,

> A shining city is perhaps all the President sees from the portico of the White House and the veranda of his ranch, where everyone seems to be doing well.
>
> But there's another city, there's another part to the shining city, the part where some people can't pay their mortgages and most young people can't afford one, where students can't afford the education they need and middle-class parents watch the dreams they hold for their children evaporate.
>
> In this part of the city there are more poor than ever, more families in trouble. More and more people who need help but can't find it. . . .
>
> And there are people who sleep in the city's streets, in the gutter, where the glitter doesn't show (Cuomo, 1984).

The new urban homeless are those who have fallen through the cracks of a social structure that is being profoundly shaken and reshaped by long-term economic and social trends and current political policies. The causes of homelessness in the 1980s are to be found not only in individual deviance and pathology, such as personal instability, drug and alcohol dependence, mental illness, or a lack of "marketable" job skills or "correct" social attitudes, but primarily in the major social, economic and political processes that are transforming our society and the unwillingness of the government to guarantee shelter for those who are the victims of this transformation.

Lawyers for the homeless in Los Angeles have contended that the right to shelter is the basis of all constitutional rights. Life, liberty, and the pursuit of happiness are difficult to conceive without the essential lifeline of basic shelter. This is why the problem of homelessness may be the leading human rights issue for the United States in the latter part of the 1980s.

To blame the victims and attribute their plight to personal failure denies reality, when in fact the actual sources of the problem are decreases in available low-income housing, housing discrimination, structural unemployment caused by deindustrialization of basic industry, job discrimination, and cutbacks in social welfare. The problems of the homeless will not be resolved if we continue to give credence to erroneous "blaming-the-victim" explanations and to base social programs on such false perspectives.

REFERENCES

Abrams, G. (1986, November 16). The reweaver of L.A.'s skid row safety net: Redevelopment chief at the center of hotel controversy. *Los Angeles Times* (Pt. 4), p. 1.

Abrams, G. (1987a, January 25). For the homeless in LA., survival can be a full time job. *Los Angeles Times* (Pt. 4), p. 1.

Abrams, G. (1987b, June 4). Homeless crackdown spurs rush to hotels: Housing agency accused of aggravating problem, moving slowly to provide shelter. *Los Angeles Times*, View Section, p. 1.

Ackerman, T. (1985, May 13). Justiceville closed, residents arrested. *Los Angeles Downtown News*, pp. 3, 20.

Anderson, C. (1974). *Toward a new sociology* (Rev. ed.). Illinois: Dorsey Press.

Aneshensel, C. (1985). The natural history of depressive symptoms: Implication for psychiatric epidemiology. In J. Greenley (Ed.), *Research in community and mental health* (Vol. 5). Greenwich, CT: JAI Press.

Arce, A., Tadlock, M., Vergare, M., & Shapiro, S. (1983). A psychiatric profile of street people admitted to an emergency shelter. *Hospital and Community Psychiatry*, 34(9), 812–817.

Arce, A., & Vergare, M. (1984). Identifying and characterizing the mentally ill among the homeless. In H. R. Lamb (Ed.), *The homeless mentally ill: A task force report of the American Psychiatric Association*. Washington, DC: American Psychiatric Association.

Babbie, E. (1973). *Survey research methods*. Belmont, CA: Wadsworth.

Babbie, E. (1975). *The practice of social research*. Belmont, CA: Wadsworth.

Bachrach, L. (1984). Interpreting research on the homeless mentally ill: Some caveats. *Hospital and Community Psychiatry, 35*(9), 914–916.

Bahr, H. (1973). *Skid row: An introduction to disaffiliation*. New York: Oxford University Press.

Bahr, H., & Caplow, T. (1974). *Old men drunk and sober*. New York: New York University Press.

Bahr, H., & Houts, K. (1971). Can you trust an homeless man? A comparison of official records and interview responses by Bowery men. *Public Opinion Quarterly, 35*, 374–382.

Bannister v. Los Angeles County Board of Supervisors (1985). Case No. C535833, Superior Court of the State of California.

Bassuk, E. (1984a). The homelessness problem. *Scientific American, 251*(1), 40–45.

Bassuk, E. (1984b). Is homelessness a mental health problem? *American Journal of Psychiatry, 41*(12), 1546–1549.

Bassuk, E. (Ed.). (1986a). *The mental health needs of homeless persons*. San Francisco: Jossey-Bass.

Bassuk, E. (1986b, February 10). A psychiatrist to the poor tells the tale of the uprooted life of families and the friendless. Interview in *People*, p. 88.

Bassuk, E., & Lamb, H. R. (1986). Homelessness and the implementation of deinstitutionalization. In E. Bassuk (Ed.), *The mental health needs of homeless persons* (pp. 7–14). San Francisco: Jossey-Bass.

Bassuk, E., Rubin, L., & Lauriot, A. (1986). Characteristics of sheltered homeless families. *American Journal of Public Health, 76*(9), 1097–1101.

Becklund, L. (1984, September 18). Building becomes a bitter battleground. *Los Angeles Times*, Metro Section, p. 1.

Belcher, J. (1983, December 25). Runaways: Slipping through the cracks and onto the streets. *Los Angeles Times*.

Belsie, L. (1986, January 9). U.S. jobs tide rises, but many workers are still aground. *Christian Science Monitor*.

Bennion v. Los Angeles County Board of Supervisors (1987). Case No. C637718, Superior Court of the State of California.

Berger, J. (1985, February 19). Failure of plan for homeless reflects city housing crisis. *New York Times*, p. 1.

Blair v. Los Angeles County Board of Supervisors (1985). Case No. C568184, Superior Court of the State of California.

Blasi, G. (1984, December 18). Testimony of Gary Blasi before the Intergovernmental Relations and Human Resources Subcommittee of the Committee on Government Relations (Mimeographed).

Blasi, G. (1985). Rights of the homeless: Litigation concerning homeless people. *Public Law Forum, 4*(2), 433–443.

Blasi, G. (1986, December). Litigation on behalf of the homeless: Systematic approaches. *Journal of Urban and Contemporary Law, 31.*

Blasi, G. (1987, June 22). Telephone conversation with the author.

Bluestone, B., & Harrison, B. (1982). *The deindustrialization of America.* New York: Basic Books.

Bodenheimer, T. (1984, July–August). The looting of America: Domestic effects of Reagan militarism. *Central America Alert, 2*, 5.

Bogue, D. (1963). *Skid row in American cities.* Chicago: University of Chicago Press.

Boyer, R., Robertson, M., & Ropers, R. (1984, November 11–15). *The homeless in Los Angeles: Demographics, homeless history, general and mental health status, health service utilization.* Paper presented at the 112th Annual Meeting of the American Public Health Association, Anaheim, CA.

Boyer, R., & Ropers, R. (1984, November 11–15). *Urban homeless drug and alcohol use and abuse.* Paper presented at the 112th Annual Meeting of the American Public Health Association, Anaheim, CA.

Bradley, T. (1984, December 18). Testimony before the Intergovernmental Relations and Human Resources Subcommittee of the Committee on Government Operations. News release, Los Angeles: Mayor's Office.

Braginsky, D., & Braginsky, B. (1975). Surplus people: Their lost faith in self and system. *Psychology Today, 9*(3), 68–73.

Breed, W. (1963). Occupational mobility and suicide among white males. *American Sociological Review, 28*, 179–188.

Brenner, H. (1976). *Estimating the social costs of national economic policy: Implications for mental and physical health and criminal aggression*

(Publication No. 76-666 0). Washington, DC: Government Printing Office.

Brenner, M. (1973). *Mental illness and the economy*. Cambridge, MA: Harvard University Press.

Brickner, P., Scharer, L., Conoran, B., Elvy, A., & Savarese, M. (Eds.). (1985). *Health care of homeless people*. New York: Springer.

Brown, C., MacFarlane, S., Parede, R., & Stark, L. (1983). *The homeless of Phoenix: Who are they? And what should be done?* Phoenix, AZ: Phoenix South Community Health Center.

Brown, J. (1987). Hunger in the U.S. *Scientific American, 256*(2), 37–41.

Bruns, R. (1980). *Knights of the road: A hobo history*. New York: Methuen.

Burns, M. (1984, September 23). Judge orders repair of "nuisance" hotel. *Los Angeles Times* (Pt. 9), p. 1.

California Employment Development Department (CEDD) (1984). *Annual planning information, Los Angeles-Long Beach SMSA, 1984–1985* (pp. 10–15). Sacramento, CA: the department.

Calmore, J. (1986). National housing policies and black America: Trends, issues, and implications. In *The state of black America in 1986*. New York: National Urban League.

Carison, T. (1985, May 10). From Justiceville to jail. *Los Angeles Herald Examiner*, p. 1.

Carison, T. (1987a, March 10). City officials work "health-and-safety" sweep. *Los Angeles Herald Examiner*, p. A1.

Carison, T. (1987b, May 29). Gates to homeless: Scram! *Los Angeles Herald Examiner*, p. 1.

Carison, T. (1987c, May 30). Don't jail homeless, Hahn says. *Los Angeles Herald Examiner*, p. A1.

Caulk, R. (1983). *The homeless poor: Multnomah County*. Portland, OR: Social Services Division.

Center on Budget and Policy Priorities (1984, September). *End results: The impact of federal policies since 1980 on low income Americans*. Washington, DC: the Center.

Chandler, J. (1987, January 30). Homeless off the hook in police scuffle. *Los Angeles Herald Examiner*.

Chavez, S., & Quinn, J. (1987, May 24). Garages: Immigrants in, cars out. *Los Angeles Times*, p. 1.

Cimons, M. (1983, August 3). 15% of Americans living in poverty, highest since 1965. *Los Angeles Times*, p. 1.

City confronts "bombshell." (1983, July 10). *Los Angeles Times*, Metro Section, p. 1.

City of Chicago (1983). *Homelessness in Chicago*. Chicago: Social Services Task Force, City of Chicago Department of Human Services.

Clarke, G. J. (1979). In defense of deinstitutionalization. *Health and Society*, *57*(4), 461–479.

Clem, W. (1984). Declaration of William Clem, MD. In Ross v. Los Angeles County Board of Supervisors. Case No. C501603 (unpublished exhibit), Superior Court of the State of California.

Clifford, F., & Clayton, J. (1987, February 25). Bradley seeks to distance himself from raid policy. *Los Angeles Times*, p. 1.

Connell, R., & Dolan, M. (1985, January 3). As tent city falls, county affirms policy. *Los Angeles Times*, Metro Section, pp. 1, 6.

Cross, W. T., & Cross, D. E. (1937). *Newcomers & nomads in California*. Stanford, CA: Stanford University Press.

Crystal, S., & Goldstein, M. (1984a). *Correlates of shelter utilization: One-day study*. New York: City of New York, Human Resources Administration.

Crystal, S., & Goldstein, M. (1984b). *The homeless in New York City shelters*. New York: City of New York, Human Resources Administration.

Cuomo, M. (1983, July). *1933–1983—Never again, a report to the National Governors Association Task Force on the Homeless* (p. 42). In *Homelessness in America II* (Serial No. 98–64). Washington, DC: Government Printing Office.

Cuomo, M. (1984). Keynote address. *Official proceedings of the 1984 Democratic National Convention*. Washington, DC: Democratic National Committee.

Cusolito, K. (1987, June 4). Haven for homeless besides jail. *Los Angeles Herald Examiner*.

Decker, C. (1987, February 1). Ted Hayes. *Los Angeles Times*, Metro Section (Pt. 2), p. 1.

de Wolfe, E. (1982, April 25). Hotels vanishing as living space for 10,000 people. *Los Angeles Times* (Pt. 8), p. 1.

de Wolfe, E. (1984, July 8). Women's center acquires site: Renovated facility to house skid row's destitute. *Los Angeles Times*.

Diagnostic and statistical manual of mental disorders (DSM) (3rd ed.). (1980). Washington, DC: American Psychiatric Association.

Dohrenwend, B. P., & Dohrenwend, B. S. (1969). *Social status and psychological disorder: A caused inquiry*. New York: Wiley.

Dohrenwend, B. P., & Dohrenwend, B. S. (1982). Perspectives on the past and future of psychiatric epidemiology. (Rema Lapouse Lecture). *American Journal of Public Health, 72*, 1271.

Dolan, M. (1984, December 23). Tent city for homeless dramatizes their plight: Life under the big top—damp but cozy. *Los Angeles Times* (Pt. 2), pp. 1, 3.

Dolcemascolo, M. A. (1985, June 21–27). Justiceville people have a recurring nightmare. *Los Angeles Weekly* (picture and caption), p. 6.

Dooley, D., & Catalano, R. (1980). Economic change as a cause of behavioral disorder. *Psychological Bulletin, 87*, 450–468.

Eckhardt, K., & Ermann, M. (1977). *Social research methods: Perspective, theory and analysis.* New York: Random House.

Edelstein, B. (1985, April 17). "Justiceville" given reprieve. *Wave* (Los Angeles, CA).

Eisenberg, P., & Lazarsfeld, P. (1938). The psychological effects of unemployment. *Psychological Bulletin, 35*, 358–390.

Eisenheim v. Los Angeles County Board of Supervisors (1983). Case No. C479453, Superior Court of the State of California.

Engels, F. (1973). *The condition of the working class in England: From personal observations and authentic sources.* (1st ed. 1844). Moscow: Progress Publishers.

Failure of the city side east "leadership" also scored. (1987). *LOVE: The Magazine of the Los Angeles Union of the Homeless, Inc., 1*(2), 2.

Farr, R. (1982). Skid row project (Mimeographed). Los Angeles: Los Angeles County Department of Mental Health, Program Development Bureau.

Farr, R. (1983). *The Los Angeles skid row mental health project.* Los Angeles: Los Angeles County Department of Mental Health, Program Development Bureau.

Farr, R. (1986). A mental health treatment program for the homeless mentally ill in the Los Angeles skid row area. In B. Jones (Ed.), *Treating the homeless: Urban psychiatry's challenge* (pp. 65–92). Washington, DC: American Psychiatric Press.

Farr, R., Koegel, P., & Burnam, A. (1986). *A study of homelessness and mental illness in the skid row area of Los Angeles.* Los Angeles: Los Angeles County Department of Mental Health.

Federationist. (1979, October). Monthly magazine of AFL-CIO.

Fillenbaum, G. (1979). Social context and self-assessments of health among the elderly. *Journal of Health and Social Behavior, 20*, 45.

Fink, M. (1986, December 29). It wasn't ready in time for Christmas, but shelter for the homeless is never too late at Tent City II. *Los Angeles Herald Examiner*, p. A3.

Fischer, P., & Breakey, W. (1986). Homelessness and mental health: An overview. *International Journal of Mental Health, 14*(4), 6–41.

Fischer, P., Shapiro, S., & Anthony, J. (1983, November 13–17). *Sociodemographic and health characteristics of transients.* Paper presented at the 111th Annual Meeting of the American Public Health Association, Dallas, TX.

Fischer, P., Shapiro, S., Breakey, W., Anthony, J., & Kramer, M. (1986). Mental health and social characteristics of the homeless: A survey of mission users. *American Journal of Public Health, 76*(5), 519–523.

Fitch, L. (1985, March 4). Suit claims welfare penalty is "barbaric." *Los Angeles Downtown News*, p. 1.

Freedom of choice. (1987, February). *Time*, p. 23.

Freeman, P. (1984, April 15). The dispossessed: Take a look at the homeless, you could be one of them. *Los Angeles Herald Examiner*, California Living Section.

Furillo, A. (1984, October 12). Slum court may go after L.A. landlords. *Los Angeles Times*, p. 3.

General Accounting Office, U.S. (GAO) (1985). *Homeless: A complex problem and the federal response.* (GAO/HRD–85–40). Washington, DC: GAO.

Goldin, G. (1986, August 29–September 4). SROpportunism: Andy Raubeson's skid row clean-up organization is a slumlord. *L.A. Weekly.*

Goldman, H. H., Adams, N., & Taube, C. (1983). Deinstitutionalization: The data demythologized. *Hospital and Community Psychiatry, 34*(2), 129–134.

Goldstein, M., Siegel, Jr., & Boyer, R. (1984). Predicting changes in perceived health status. *American Journal of Public Health, 74*, 611.

Goleman, D. (1985, April 23). State hospital accused of wrong diagnoses, fueling debate over nation's mental care. *New York Times*, Science Times, p. 19.

Goleman, D. (1986, November 4). To expert eyes, city streets are open mental wards. *New York Times*, p. C1.

Hansen v. Los Angeles County Board of Supervisors (1986). Case No. CA974, Superior Court of the State of California.

Harrington, M. (1984). *The new American poverty*. New York: Holt, Rinehart & Winston.

Hartman, C. (1982). Housing. In A. Gartner, C. Greer & F. Riessman (Eds.), *What Reagan is doing to us* (p. 141). New York: Harper & Row.

Hartman, C. (Ed.) (1983). *America's housing crisis: What is to be done?* Boston: Routledge & Kegan Paul.

Hartman, C. (1986). Housing policies under the Reagan administration. In R. Bratt, C. Hartman, & A. Meyerson (Eds.), *Critical perspectives on housing* (pp. 362–376). Philadelphia: Temple University Press.

Hastings, D. (1983a, July 25). Owner of skid row hotel may face city prosecution. *Los Angeles Times*, Metro Section, p. 1.

Hastings, D. (1983b, August 1). Skid row task force. *Los Angeles Times*, Metro Section, p. 1.

Hayes, T. (1985, June 9). Q & A: Minister exhorts L.A. to give justice to the homeless [interview]. *Los Angeles Herald Examiner*, p. C4.

Health and Human Services, U.S. Department of (1983). *Alcohol and health: Fifth special report to the U.S. Congress*. Rockville, MD: Author.

Health, Education, & Welfare, U.S. Dept. of (HEW) (1973). *Work in America, A Report of a special task force to the Secretary*. Cambridge, MA: MIT Press.

Henry, H. (1955). *Mission on main street*. Los Angeles: Union Rescue Mission Press.

Hernandez, M. (1984, October 23). Repair work begins on burned mission. *Los Angeles Times* (Pt. 2), p. 1.

Hernandez, M., & Wolinsky, L. (1984, December 27). Downtown's tent city for homeless wins 1-week extension. *Los Angeles Times* (Pt. 2), pp. 1, 6.

Heskin, A. (1984). *Availability of overnight housing at/under $10.00 per night in the Los Angeles County market*. Unpublished paper, Los Angeles: UCLA School of Architecture and Urban Planning.

Hispanic poverty rate near that of blacks (1986, September 4). *New York Times*, p. A14.

Hollingshead, A., & Redlich, F. (1958). *Social class and mental illness: A community study*. New York: Wiley.

Hombs, M. E., & Snyder, M. (1983). *Homelessness in America: A forced march to nowhere*. Washington, DC: Community for Creative Non-Violence.

Homeless aid gets boost from house leaders. (1987, January 17). *Congressional Quarterly*, pp. 121–123.

Homeless by choice? Some choice (1984, February 7). *New York Times*, p. A24.

Homelessness in L.A. up 50%, biggest rise in U.S. (1987, January 25). *Los Angeles Times* (Pt. 4), p. 8.

Hopper, K., Baxter, E., Cox, S., & Klein, L. (1982). *One year later: The homeless poor in New York City*. New York: Community Service Society.

Hopper, K., & Cox, L. (1982). *Litigation in advocacy for the homeless: The case of New York City*. New York: Coalition for the Homeless.

Hopper, K., & Hamberg, J. (1986). The making of America's homeless: From skid row to new poor, 1945–1984. In R. Bratt, C. Hartman, & A. Meyerson (Eds.), *Critical perspectives on housing* (pp. 12–40). Philadelphia: Temple University Press.

Housing and Urban Development, U.S. Dept. of (HUD). (1984). *A report to the secretary on the homeless and emergency shelters*. Washington, DC: HUD Office of Policy Development and Research.

Hurst, J. (1986, June 8). Houses of horror: "Slum busters" cracking down on dangerous, dilapidated apartments. *Los Angeles Times*, Metro Section.

Ille, M. (1980). *Burnside: A study of hotel residents in Portland's skid road*. Portland: The Burnside Consortium.

Jacob, J. (1986). Overviewing black America in 1985. In *The State of Black America in 1986*. New York: National Urban League.

Johnston, O. (1983, December 3). Jobless rate soars to 7.5%; Data disputed. *Los Angeles Times*, p. 1.

Jones, B. (Ed.). (1986). *Treating the homeless: Urban psychiatry's challenge*. Washington, DC: American Psychiatric Press.

Jones, B., & Gray, B. (1986). Problems in diagnosing schizophrenia and affective disorders among blacks. *Hospital and Community Psychiatry, 37*(1), 61–65.

Jones, R. (1983). Street people and psychiatry: An introduction. *Hospital and Community Psychiatry, 34*(9), 807–811.

Justiceville [video tape] (1987). Hollywood, CA: Glaser Productions.

Kaplan, G., & Camacho, T. (1983). Perceived health and mortality: A nine-year follow up of the Human Population Laboratory Cohort. *American Journal of Epidemiology, 117*, 291.

Kellog, R., Piantieri, O., Conoran, B., Doherty, P., Vicic, W., & Brickner, P. (1985). Hypertension: A screening and treatment program for the homeless. In P. Brickner, L. Scharer, B. Conoran, A. Elvy, & M. Savarese (Eds.), *Health care of homeless people*. New York: Springer.

Kelly, J. (1985). Trauma: With the example of SAN F shelter programs. In P. Brickner, L. Scharer, B. Conoran, A. Elvy, & M. Savarese (Eds.), *Health care of homeless people*. New York: Springer.

Komarovsky, M. (1940). *The unemployed man and his family*. New York: Dryden Press.

Lamb, H. R. (1982, January). The mentally ill in an urban county jail. *Archives of General Psychiatry, 39*, 17–22.

Lamb, H. R. (Ed.). (1984a). *The homeless mentally ill: A task force report of the American Psychiatric Association*. Washington, DC: American Psychiatric Association.

Lamb, H. R. (1984b). Deinstitutionalization and the homeless mentally ill. In H. R. Lamb (Ed.), *The homeless mentally ill: A task force report of the American Psychiatric Association*. Washington, DC: American Psychiatric Association.

Lamb, H. R., & Talbott, J. A. (1986, July 25). The homeless mentally ill: The perspective of the American Psychiatric Association. *Journal of the American Medical Association, 256*(4), 498–501.

Lawson, W. B. (1986). Racial and ethnic factors in psychiatric research. *Hospital and Community Psychiatry, 37*(1), 50–53.

Lee, B. (1980). The disappearance of skid row: Some ecological evidence. *Urban Affairs Quarterly, 16*(1), 81–107.

Lendrum, F. (1933). A thousand cases of attempted suicide. *American Journal of Psychiatry, 13*, 479–500.

Levinson, B. (1963). The homeless man: A psychological enigma. *Mental Hygiene, 47*, 596–599.

Life in the hotels. (1983, July 10). *Los Angeles Times*, Metro Section, p. 1.

Lipton, A., & Simon, F. (1985). Psychiatric diagnoses in a state hospital: Manhattan State revisited. *Hospital and Community Psychiatry, 36*(4), 368–372.

Lipton, F., Sabatini, A., & Katz, S. (1983). Down and out in the city: The homeless mentally ill. *Hospital and Community Psychiatry, 34*(9), 817–821.

Los Angeles Catholic Worker (1984). *Homelessness report: Strategy for survival*. Los Angeles: Author.

Los Angeles County Department of Mental Health (1982). *Concerned agencies of metropolitan Los Angeles resource directory.* Los Angeles: Author.

Los Angeles County Department of Mental Health and Department of Public Social Services (1984). *A study of the homeless and mentally ill in the Los Angeles skid row area.* Los Angeles: Author.

Los Angeles County Department of Public Social Services. (1983). *General relief recipient characteristics study.* Los Angeles: Author.

Lumsden, G. (1983). *Issues associated with housing the indigent: The Salvation Army set-up shelter program.* Dallas, TX: Department of Health and Human Services.

MacDougall, A. (1984, October 25). Rich-poor gap in U.S. widens during decade. *Los Angeles Times*, p. 1.

MacMahon, B., Johnson, S., & Pugh, R. (1963). Relation of suicide rates to social conditions: Evidence from U.S. vital statistics. *Public Health Reports, 78*, 285–293.

Maharidge, D. (1985). *Journey to nowhere: The saga of the new underclass.* Newton, MA: Dial Press.

Marcus, A., Reeder, L., Jordan, L., et al. (1980). Monitoring health status, access to health care and compliance behavior in a large urban community: A report from the Los Angeles health survey. *Medical Care, 18*, 253.

Marx, K. (1965). *Capital* (Vol. 1; 1st ed. 1867). Moscow: Progress Publisher.

Massey, J., & Shapiro, E. (1982). Self-rated health: A predictor of mortality among the elderly. *American Journal of Public Health, 72*, 800.

May, L. (1985, April 30). 325,000 jobless facing end of extended benefits. *Los Angeles Times*.

McAdams, J., Brickner, P., Glicksman, R., Edwards, D., Fallon, B., & Yanowitch, P. (1985). Tuberculosis in the SRO/homeless population. In P. Brickner, L. Scharer, B. Conoran, A. Elvy, & M. Savarese (Eds.), *Health care of homeless people.* New York: Springer.

McMillan, P. (1985, August 29). Skid row peacekeeper fights his last battle. *Los Angeles Times* (Pt. 2), pp. 1, 6.

McMillan, P. (1987a, February 25). They're keeping L.A.'s homeless on the move. *Los Angeles Times*, Metro Section, p. 1.

McMillan, P. (1987b, May 29). L.A. homeless on skid row to face arrest. *Los Angeles Times*.

McMillan, P. (1987c, June 3). Council calls for limits on plan to jail the homeless. *Los Angeles Times*, p. 1.

McMillan, P., & Ramos, G. (1987, June 5). Homeless fade away as police move in for arrests. *Los Angeles Times*, Part 1, p. 3.

"Meaning of Justiceville, The: L.A.'s homeless require shelter and support. (1985, May 14). *Los Angeles Herald Examiner*, p. A8.

Meltzer, M. (1969). *Brother, can you spare a dime? The great depression 1929–1933*. New York: Mentor.

Milburn, N., & Watts, R. (1985–86, Winter). Methodological issues in research on the homeless and the homeless mentally ill. *International Journal of Mental Health*, p. 47.

Miller, R. (1982). *The demolition of skid row*. Lexington, MA: Lexington Books.

Mullen, L. (1986, December 30). Tent City II given 5 days before it has to pull up stakes. *Los Angeles Herald Examiner*, p. A3.

Myers, J., & Weissman, M. (1980). Use of self-report symptoms scale to detect depression in a community sample. *American Journal of Psychiatry, 137*, 1081.

National Center for Health Statistics. (1983). *Bibliography on health indexes* (DHHS [PHS] 83–1250). Hyattsville, MD: Clearinghouse on Health Indexes.

Navarro, M. (1984, October 17). Homeless program passes test in rain. *San Francisco Examiner*, p. B5.

Nelson, B. (1983, October 2). Studies report mental illness in most homeless in 2 cities. *New York Times*, Section A, p. 17.

Nix, C. (1985a, November 4). In a hotel for homeless families, childhood dies young. *New York Times*, Metropolitan Report, p. 1.

Nix, C. (1985b, November 10). New York's mentally ill fear homeless shelters. *New York Times*.

Nyden, P. (1984, September). Unemployment: Its social costs. *Progressive Forensics*, pp. 8–10.

Ohio Department of Mental Health, Office of Program Evaluation and Research (1985). *Homelessness in Ohio: A study of people in need*. Columbus, OH: Author.

O'Kane, K. (1973). *Skid row: An interview survey*. Unpublished paper, UCLA.

Oliver, M. (1983, December 21). Homeless in L.A. describe mean streets: Judge orders welfare officials to provide shelter to eligible. *Los Angeles Times*, Metro Section, p. 1.

Oliver, M. (1984, June 13). County sued again on shelter for homeless. *Los Angeles Times*, Metro Section, p. 1.

Overend, W. (1983, May 1). Attempts at solutions to problems of the homeless. *Los Angeles Times*, Metro Section, p. 1.

Overend, W. (1984a, February 24). Parents of mentally ill find strength in alliance. *Los Angeles Times* (Pt. 5), p. 1.

Overend, W. (1984b, March 2). Shelter for homeless gives in to county. Won't take in new people until outbreak of dysentery clears up. *Los Angeles Times*.

Palmer, D. (1986, February 22). Psychiatrist says treatment needed by many homeless. *Deseret News* (Salt Lake City, UT).

Paris v. Los Angeles County Board of Supervisors (1984). Case No. C523361, Superior Court of California.

Persell, C. (1987). *Understanding society: An introduction to sociology.* New York: Harper & Row.

Pierce, A. (1967). The economic cycle and the social suicide rate. *American Sociological Review, 32,* 457–462.

Pinkney, A. (1984). *The myth of black progress.* Cambridge: Cambridge University Press.

Piven, F., & Cloward, R. (1971). *Regulation of the poor: The functions of public welfare.* New York: Vintage Books.

Piven, F., & Cloward, R. (1977). *Poor people's movements: Why they succeed, how they fail.* New York: Vintage Books.

Piven, F., & Cloward, R. (1982). *The new class war.* New York: Pantheon Books.

Prokop, D. (1987, June 16). Homeless say new shelter like prison. *Outlook* (Santa Monica, CA), p. A10.

Queen, S., & Mann, D. (1925). *Social pathology.* New York: Thomas Y. Crowell.

Rensch v. Los Angeles County Board of Supervisors (1986). Case No. C595155, Superior Court of California.

Riis, J. (1890). *How the other half lives: Studies among the tenements of New York.* New York: Scribner.

Riordan, T. (1987, March/April). Housekeeping at HUD: Why the homeless problem could get much, much worse. *Common Cause, 13,* 26–31.

Roberts, R., & Vernon, S. (1983). The Center for Epidemiologic Studies depression scale for research in the general population. *American Journal of Psychiatry, 140,* 41.

Robertson, M., & Cousineau, M. (1986). Health status and access to health services among the urban homeless. *American Journal of Public Health, 76,* 5.

Robertson, M., Ropers, R., & Boyer, R. (1984). Emergency shelter for the homeless in Los Angeles County. Los Angeles: UCLA School of Public Health, Basic Shelter Research Project. Also in Intergovernmental Relations and Human Resources Subcommittee of the Committee on Government Operations (1985), *The federal response to the homeless crisis* (No. 1016A, 1016B microfiche, pp. 904–983). Washington, DC: Government Printing Office.

Robertson, M., Ropers, R., & Boyer, R. (1985). The homeless in Los Angeles County: An empírical evaluation. Los Angeles: UCLA School of Public Health, Basic Shelter Research Project. Also in *The federal response to the homeless crisis* (No. 1016A, 1016B microfiche, pp. 984–1108). Washington, DC: Government Printing Office.

Robins, L., Helzer, J., Croughan, J., & Ratcliff, K. (1981). National Institute of Mental Health diagnostic interview schedule. *Archives of General Psychiatry, 38,* 381.

Roderick, K. (1984, July 21). Horse patrols ride herd on transients: City polishing its image for Olympic visitors. *Los Angeles Times,* Metro Section, p. 1.

Ropers, R. (1984a, April 11). *The urban homeless: Deinstitutionalized or disenfranchised?* Paper presented at the 55th Annual Meeting of the Pacific Sociological Association, session on Sociology of Mental Health and Mental Disorders, Seattle, WA.

Ropers, R. (1984b, Nov. 10). *Typology and profile of the homeless.* Anaheim, CA: Conference on Homelessness in the U.S., American Public Health Association.

Ropers, R. (1984c, Nov. 10). *Theoretical model for homelessness: From social disaffiliation to "skid row" way of life.* Conference on Homelessness in the U.S., American Public Health Association. Anaheim, CA.

Ropers, R. (1985a). The contribution of economic and political policies and trends to the rise of the new urban homeless. In Intergovernmental Relations and Human Resources Subcommittee of the Committee on Government Operations, *The federal response to the homeless crisis* (No. 1016A, 1016B microfiche, pp. 833–856). Washington, DC: Government Printing Office.

Ropers, R. (1985b, December). The rise of the new urban homeless. *Public Affairs Report, 26*(5&6). Berkeley: University of California, Institute of Governmental Studies.

Ropers, R. (1986, November). *Blacks and other minorities among the homeless* (Working Paper Series). Chicago: Urban League.

Ropers, R., & Boyer, R. (1987a). Perceived health status among the new urban homeless. *International Journal of Social Science and Medicine, 24*(8), 669–678.

Ropers, R., & Boyer, R. (1987b). Homelessness as a health risk. *Alcohol Health and Research World, 11*, 38–41. Rockville, MD: U.S. Department of Health and Human Services.

Ropers, R., & Marks, T. (1983, March). *Unemployment resource handbook: Making it through the tough times.* Los Angeles: Didi Hirsch Community Mental Health Center/Los Angeles Psychiatric Services.

Ropers, R., & Robertson, M. (1984a). The inner-city homeless of Los Angeles: An empirical assessment. Los Angeles: UCLA School of Public Health, Basic Shelter Research Project. Also in *The federal response to the homeless crisis* (No. 1016A, 1016B, microfiche, pp. 858–903). Washington, DC: Government Printing Office.

Ropers, R., & Robertson, M. (1984b). *Notes on the epidemiology of homeless persons: Methodological issues.* Los Angeles: UCLA School of Public Health, Basic Shelter Research Project.

Ropers, R., & Scott, W. (1980, October 16). *Unemployment and its consequences for self and family stability.* Paper presented at 9th annual Brigham Young University Family Research Conference.

Ross v. Los Angeles County Board of Supervisors (1984). Case No. C501603, Superior Court of California.

Ryan, W. (1971). *Blaming the victim.* New York: Vintage Books.

Safety Network. (1987, September). Pres. Signs Homeless Bill; Law Funds $1 Bill. in Aid. New York: National Coalition for the Homeless, p. 1.

Salinsbury, P. (1956). *Suicide in London: An ecological study.* New York: Basic Books.

Scull, R., & Lamb, H. (1984). Deinstitutionalization and public policy (Mimeographed). Los Angeles: University of Southern California.

Shaffer, D. (1984). *Runaway and homeless youth in New York City.* New York: New York State Psychiatric Institute, Division of Child Psychiatry.

Silvern, P., & Schmunk, R. (1981). *Residential hotels in Los Angeles: A case of benign neglect.* Los Angeles: Skid Row Development Corporation.

Simon, R., & Himmel, N. (1987, January 21). L.A. opens city hall as shelter for homeless. *Los Angeles Times*, pp. 1, 16.

Singer, E., Garfinkel, R., & Cohen, S. (1976). Mortality and mental health evidences from the midtown Manhattan restudy. *Social Sciences and Medicine, 10,* 517.

Skid row pavilions. (1987, June 29). *Time*, p. 19.

Snapshot of a changing America. (1985, September 2). *Time*, p. 16.

Sontag, S. (1979). *Illness as a metaphor.* New York: Vintage Books.

Srole, L., Langer, T., & Michael, S. (1962). *Mental health in the metropolis: The midtown Manhattan study* (Vol. 1). New York: McGraw-Hill.

Stambler, L. (1984, June 14). Homeless woman wins: Ticket for sleeping in car thrown out. *Los Angeles Times.*

Swinton, D. (1986). Economic status of blacks, 1985. In *The state of Black America in 1986.* New York: National Urban League.

Szymanski, A. (1983). *Class structure: A critical perspective.* New York: Praeger.

Talbott, J. A., & Lamb, H. R. (1984). Summary and recommendations. In H. R. Lamb (Ed.), *The homeless mentally ill: A task force report of the American Psychiatric Association.* Washington, DC: American Psychiatric Association.

Taylor, D. (1984). Toward the promised land: Twenty years after passage of the Civil Rights Act, one expert sees an uneven pattern of progress and federal enforcement. *Psychology Today, 18*(6), 46–50.

Theorell, T., Lind, E., & Floderus, B. (1975). The relationship of disturbing life-changes and emotions to the early development of myocardial infarctions and other serious illness. *International Journal of Epidemiology, 4,* 281–293.

Tiffany, D., Cowan, J., & Tiffany, P. (1970). *The unemployed.* Englewood Cliffs: Prentice-Hall.

Townsend, D. (1983, July 10). Dealing with the children living in skid row. *Los Angeles Times*, Metro Section, p. 1.

Trouble in paradise: A look at L.A.'s homeless [video tape] (1986). Hollywood, CA: Glaser Productions.

Tuckman, J., & Lavell, M. (1958). Study of suicide in Philadelphia. *Public Health Reports, 73,* 547–553.

Tuohy, W. (1985, February 9). Homeless: A problem in Europe too. *Los Angeles Times*, p. 1.

United States Conference of Mayors (1986a). *The growth of hunger, homelessness and poverty in America's cities in 1985: A 25 city survey.* Washington, DC: Author.

United States Conference of Mayors (1986b). *The continued growth of hunger, homelessness and poverty in America's cities: 1986.* Washington, DC: Author.

United States Conference of Mayors (1987). *A status report on homeless families in America's cities.* Washington, DC: Author.

U.S. Congress, Joint Economic Committee (1984). *The President's 1984 national urban policy report* (pp. 39–43). Washington, DC: Government Printing Office.

U.S. Department of Commerce, Bureau of the Census (1982). *Summary characteristics for governmental units and standard metropolitan statistical areas* (California PHC 80–361). Washington, DC: Author.

U.S. Department of Labor. (1985, July). Displaced workers, 1979–83. Bureau of Labor Statistics, bulletin No. 2240. Washington, DC: Government Printing Office.

U.S. House, Committee on Banking, Finance, & Urban Affairs, Subcommittee on Housing & Development (1983). *Homelessness in America.* Washington, DC: Government Printing Office.

U.S. House, Committee on Government Operations (1985). *The federal response to the homeless crisis: Third report.* Washington, DC: Government Printing Office.

U.S. House, Committee on Ways and Means, Subcommittees on Oversight and on Public Assistance and Unemployment Compensation (1983). *Background material on poverty.* Washington, DC: Government Printing Office.

U.S. Senate, Special Committee on Aging (1978). *Single room occupancy: A need for national concern.* Washington, DC: Government Printing Office.

United Way (1983). *Emergency assistance programs exploratory survey.* Los Angeles: United Way Research Department, Planning and Allocation Division.

Vander Kooi, R. (1971). The main stem: Skid row revisited. In I. L. Horowitz & C. Nanry (Eds.), *Sociological Realities II.* New York: Harper & Row.

Vatz, R., Weinberg, L., & Szasz, T. (1985, September 15). Why does television grovel at the altar of psychiatry? *Washington Post.*

Vigderhous, G., & Fishman, G. (1978). The impact of unemployment and social integration on changing suicide rates in the U.S.A., 1920–1969. *Social Psychology, 13,* 239–248.

Wallace, S. (1965). *Skid row as a way of life.* Totowa, NJ: Bedminster Press.

Ware, J., Davis-Avery, A., & Donald, C. (1978). *Conceptualization and measurement of health for adults in the health insurance study,* Vol. 5, *General health perceptions.* Santa Monica: Rand.

Warner, R. (1985). *Recovery from schizophrenia: Psychiatry and political economy.* London: Routledge & Kegan Paul.

Waters, R. (1984). *Trickle-down tragedy: Homelessness in California.* Sacramento: California Homeless Coalition.

Weissman, M. (1975). Comparison of a self-report symptom rating scale (CES-D) with standardized depression rating scales in psychiatric populations. *American Journal of Epidemiology, 102,* 430.

Wilcock, R., & Franke, W. (1963). *Unwanted workers.* New York: Free Press.

Wilson, W. (1985). The black community in the 1980s: Questions of race, class, and public policy. In Finsterbusch (Ed.), *Sociology 85/86* (pp. 169–176). Guilford, CT: Dushkin.

Wilson, W. (1986, March 3). Quoted in Debating plight of the urban poor. *U.S. News and World Report,* pp. 21–22.

Zasada, M. (1986, March 3). Shelter them in lobbies, basements, hallways. *Los Angeles Downtown News,* p. 1.

Ziegler, J. (1986, January 22). Racial differences pose problems. *Daily Spectrum* (Iron County, UT, edition), p. B2.

LIST OF TABLES AND FIGURES

INDEX